By Resolution and Perseverance

By Resolution and Perseverance:

The History of the Humane Society of the Commonwealth of Massachusetts

By John Galluzzo

"To all humane societies."

Table of Contents

Introduction   i
It Took a Blind Man to See   1
A Small Step   13
Rapid Growth   23
Action   29
Opportunity Lost   39
Interregnum   45
Right Man for the Job   55
Into the Golden Age   67
A New Breed of Hero   75
Onto the National Scene   85
Dedicated to the Cause   95
Forgotten Hero   107
The Price   117
End of an Era   123
Epilogue   129
Postscript   139
Acknowledgments   143

Introduction

After nearly a half a century of lifesaving along the shores of the town of Hull, the volunteer lifeboat crews of the Humane Society of the Commonwealth of Massachusetts were about to be joined by the federal government in their battle with the unscrupulous fury of wind and wave of New England winter storms. The earliest lifeboat crews, under Captain Moses Binney Tower, launched into the breakers in search of shipwreck survivors in 1840. In October of 1888, one of Tower's young crewmen, Joshua James, now in his sixties, was still at it, taking up the sweep oar as the keeper of the Humane Society's boats in Hull.

According to the *Hingham Journal* of October 26, 1888, the United States Life-Saving Service had finally decided to take up position at the mouth of Boston Harbor, to supplement, or even replace, the volunteer crews. "Proposals were opened last week in Washington," read the *Journal*, "for the construction of the Point Allerton, Hull life-saving station, and which will be in commission before the end of next summer." The brief article went on to describe the building, of standard design used elsewhere in the country. "The rooms are all spacious and well ventilated, and every provision has been made for the health and comfort of the men."

The Life-Saving Service, under the guidance of General Superintendent Sumner Increase Kimball, arrived in Massachusetts in 1872, locating nine stations along the coast of Cape Cod. Several

South Shore of Boston villages had seen their volunteer lifesaving efforts augmented by "the government's hired men" in the ensuing years: Plymouth, at the Gurnet and at Manomet Point in 1874; Scituate, at Fourth Cliff in 1879 and North Scituate in 1886. Yet the Hull men, tasked with guarding the busy shipping lanes of Lighthouse Channel, heading into and out of the city of Boston, between Boston Light and the northern shores of Hull, remained unaided by the federal government's growing network of stations and up-to-date equipment. The *Hingham Journal* of November 23, 1888, (the day after Joshua James' 62nd birthday) reported the big news that "Superintendent Kimball of the Life-Saving Service has made the award for the construction of the life-saving station, at Point Allerton, Hull...The station will be fully equipped and in running order by next winter."

Mother Nature was apparently not amused.

The following afternoon, a storm, described by the locals as the most powerful natural event since the Minot's Light Gale of April 16-17, 1851, slammed the Massachusetts coastline, began to unleash its wrath. The next morning, on Sunday, November 25, Captain Joshua James scaled the heights of Telegraph Hill at the northern end of the seven mile Hull peninsula and scanned the surrounding waters for ships potentially in danger. "Vessels anchored off the Lighthouse Channel, about ½ mile southwest of Boston Light, could easily be seen, and, as near as I do now remember," he would later tell Lieutenant Oscar C. Hamlet of the U.S. Revenue Marine, "there were five schooners and one coal barge in a position exposed to the sea and east gale."

At about two p.m., James and a crew of volunteers made ready the lifeboat *R.B. Forbes*, dragging it from its Stony Beach boathouse to a position he felt some of the distressed vessels might come ashore, ordering also that the boat *Robert G. Shaw* be moved from the Point Allerton boathouse to Stony Beach. At nearly that same time, the three-masted schooner *Cox and Green* of Greenpoint, New York, laden with seven hundred tons of coal bound for Chelsea, Massachusetts, ran aground just west of the Toddy Rocks, north of Telegraph Hill. The Humane Society volunteers rushed to action, bringing the lifeboat and a beach apparatus cart, loaded with the elements of the breeches buoy rescue device, to the scene.

Any lifeboat launch would be treacherous, owing to the field of partially submerged rocks that gave the locale its name, and James concluded as well that "the sea was so heavy that I considered it too risky to launch the boat." Fortuitously, after the *Cox and Green*'s chains had parted, the schooner had drifted within range of the Hunt line-throwing gun, used to rig a breeches buoy apparatus.

Many of the local townsfolk turned out to help with the rescue, which involved firing a line to the ship, sending out a hawser, breeches buoy (canvas pants sewn onto a life ring and suspended by four ropes from a traveling block that rode on the hawser), and other equipment to the ship, digging a hole and burying a sand anchor, and, among other tasks, hauling on lines to pull the mariners ashore one at a time.

With the seas smashing the broadsides of the schooner, the crew of nine men had taken to the rigging. Having anchored in Nantasket Roads at 11:30 p.m., Captain Henry Thompson had watched the gale increase during the early morning hours, and he and his crew witnessed their foresail and forestaysail tear away in the wind. They had dragged anchor around noon and run aground at 2 p.m., just moments before the lifesavers arrived. Joshua James and his army of volunteers pulled them all to safety with relative ease, the rescue running as smoothly as could be anticipated, with the unpredictable element of the weather in charge of the day's events. Local resident J. William Smith opened his doors to the survivors, offering them a place to warm up and wind down.

Before the last man had landed on firm ground, though, James and his lifesavers took note of another vessel coming ashore about an eighth of a mile to the east of the *Cox and Green*. The three-masted schooner *Gertrude Abbott*, with 825 tons of coal headed from Philadelphia to Boston, had struck the rocks hard, seemingly beyond the reach of the Hunt gun. The captain, John Thompson, ordered the American ensign flown upside-down, a recognized call for help from ashore. The volunteers moved their equipment up the beach to the scene and dug a pit for the placement of the sand anchor, but James ultimately concluded the rescue would need to be effected by use of the lifeboat.

Now fighting the darkness allying with the storm, and with the tide approaching its highest point, James directed his men to build a large bonfire atop Souther's Hill, a bluff overlooking the disaster scene. The lifesavers waited for the tide to ebb, but due to the fury of the storm, no noticeable lull or change occurred. The Captain discussed the dangers of the impending rescue with his men. "Captain James warned his crew that the chances were they would never return from the attempt to save the shipwrecked men," wrote Sumner Kimball in his 1909 biography of James, "but asked who were willing to go with him and make the effort." James later related that he felt "the danger of the crew of the vessel was also fully understood if a rescue was not attempted on the next low tide." His men faced a grave choice: risk their own lives now so others might live, or wait out the storm and know that the shipwrecked sailors would probably die. Some of the volunteers turned their lifejackets over to others from the crowd who were willing to face the odds, and the lifeboat filled with would-be lifesavers.

The trip seaward, taken between 8 and 9 p.m., was as dangerous as James imagined it would be. Having grown up on the beaches and waters of Hull, he knew every sunken stone, every protruding rock like a brother. "The boat was repeatedly filled," wrote Kimball, "as the huge waves swept over it, disputing every inch of the way and often forcing it back into imminent peril of being dashed to pieces on the rocks." Two men were detailed to do nothing but bail water out of the boat, as the seas, "running mountain high," continuously assaulted the *R.B. Forbes* and its crew as they battled their way through the breakers.

After a strenuous pull, the lifeboat arrived alongside the *Gertrude Abbott*. The lifesavers tossed a heaving line aboard the schooner, which the ship's crew made fast on deck. One by one, the sailors tied the ropes about their waists and timed their leaps with the crests of the waves, diving with fragile faith into the outstretched arms of the tired, wet and cold lifesavers below. Eight times over this pageant played out, each man finding temporary safety from the storm in the arms of his fellow men, until the entire crew had made the jump.

Now, though, with the R. B. Forbes weighted down with twice as much humanity as on its trip to the wreck, the lifesavers turned to the task of returning to shore and navigating the Toddy Rocks with the surging waves pushing them from behind. Hindered by the presence of the eight survivors, the lifesavers worked the oars as best they could, but the storm soon took the upper hand. About 600 feet from shore, the boat struck a rock and rolled to one side. Oars flew away and one of the lifesavers was tossed from the boat. The crew shifted their combined weight to windward and righted the craft, simultaneously pulling their displaced fellow lifesavers back aboard. "I called to the men as loudly as I could to stick to the boat," related James, "no matter what might happen."

Those words, of course, were easier understood than adhered to under the current circumstances. The boat crashed toward the shore, alternately hitting rocks and being swung through green water at the whim of the sea, all the while the lifesavers using what few oars were left to push the R. B. Forbes free of obstructions and on a general course toward the beach. "It seemed like a miracle that she was not thrown bottom up by some of the breakers when striking the rocks," said James.

Finally, though, such a situation unfolded. The boat struck a rock that opened a gaping hole in the starboard side, but the lifesavers and their rescued charges realized they were in shoal water, and close enough to the shore to scramble to safety. This time, Mrs. Esther Reed beckoned the survivors to her home, where they found warmth, food and comfortable beds for the evening.

As the Cox and Green and Gertrude Abbott survivors slept, the Humane Society volunteers patrolled the beaches in the dark, keeping sharp eyes out for more trouble, as the storm mercilessly continued its battering of the ships at anchor along the shore. "Often they had to wade deep gullies, with difficulty avoiding the wreckage that was thrashing about in the surf," wrote Kimball, "and now and again they had to run for their lives to escape an exceptionally high sea that chased them up the beach and threatened to engulf them." At 3 a.m., just six hours after the rescue of the Gertrude Abbott's sailors had ended, a patrolling lifesaver spotted a third vessel, the three-masted schooner *Bertha Walker* of Taunton, Massachusetts, carrying 975 tons of coal into the city of Boston from Philadelphia.

The *Bertha Walker*'s story mirrored that of the *Gertrude Abbott*. "We arrived in the Roads and anchored at midnight Saturday, after an uneventful trip," an unidentified crewmember told the *Hingham Journal* after the storm abated. "The storm came up, but we rode it out all right till about 1 o'clock Sunday noon, when we dragged, and after drifting about all the afternoon we struck on the beach at about 10 p.m."

Visibility had deteriorated so badly during the evening hours that the lifesavers did not find the ship for five hours. From 10 p.m. until 1 a.m., the crew huddled below the forecastle deck, but when the seas began to break over that part of the vessel, the crew scrambled for the rigging. The captain and first mate stayed below until they were sure the others were secure, but paid for their dedication to their crew when a wave swept them off the deck to their deaths.

James and the lifesavers knew they did not stand a chance of enacting a successful rescue in the dark. In fact, Captain James, a veteran of nearly fifty years of storm fighting, dating back to his teen years, declared this storm one of the worst he had ever encountered. "It was raining heavy and blowing harder," he said, "than I had seen it blow for years."

At daybreak, the weary lifesavers could see the seven remaining crewmen in the rigging of the *Bertha Walker*, a half mile northwest of the *Gertrude Abbott*. James arranged for the *Robert G. Shaw* to be pulled by horse and carriage from Stony Beach to Pemberton Point, allowing for the lifesavers to launch their lifeboat from inside the peninsula, thereby avoiding the pounding surf altogether. Rowing out through Hull Gut – the same stretch of water in which 10 year-old Joshua James had watched his mother die fifty-one years earlier – the volunteers headed for the wreck off Toddy Rocks. After a long and draining pull toward the ship, James examined the situation.

As the schooner had stabilized amongst the rocks, the only danger to the lifesavers came in positioning themselves alongside the stricken ship. Each approaching wave struck the seaward side of the vessel with explosive force, breaking over both the bow and the stern, but the lifesavers and the seven crewmen timed the rescue with choreographed precision. A wave would smash the vessel's side, and as it ebbed, a survivor would drop into the lifeboat; another wave would then hit, and as it receded, another survivor would make his way into the smaller vessel.

As John R. Spearwater whisked the survivors to the Pemberton Hotel, James spied another vessel flying a distress signal out off Toddy Rocks. He requested the aid of a nearby tugboat, wanting to save the strength of his men, and approached the schooner, the *Puritan* of Boston. The ship was in no immediate danger, but requested a tow in to port. When James and the crew returned to Pemberton Wharf for a second time, a messenger on horseback alerted them that yet another ship had come ashore, six miles to the south, at Atlantic Hill.

By now, James and many of the men working with him – his son Osceola, members of the Mitchell, Galiano, Pope, Lowe and Smith families, among others – had been rowing, patrolling the beaches and changing the course of destiny for ships full of men for approximately eighteen hours. And, for the most part, they had done so without food of any kind, as the storm saw no reason to stop and wait for meals to be consumed.

They proceeded to the scene of the next wreck. "As this was on the outside beach," said James, "I concluded to take the large surfboat *Nantasket* which had been carried across from Station No. 20, and towed up Weir River with the same tug. We landed on the narrow beach, inside of Hotel Nantasket, hauled the boat over, launched on the other side and pulled along inside of the breakers to get abreast of the vessel." The *Nantasket*, an original and unusual design by Joshua's older brother Samuel James, would be tested for the first time on this day, Monday, November 26, 1888. But before a single victim could be coaxed to find refuge between its gunwales, *Nantasket* received its first wounds in the war against Poseidon's rage. "We had to make a landing in order to haul the boat over a narrow point of land," recounted James, "and launch again on the other side of it. While making the landing, the boat was stove in on

The Mattie E. Eaton, *wrecked on Nantasket Beach during the Great Storm of November 1888, was but one of six wrecks to which Humane Society crews responded in Hull during the tempest (Courtesy of Dick Boonisar).*

the rocks, but temporary repairs were soon made and lead patches put over the holes."

Heading from Hillsboro, Nova Scotia, for Newberg, New York, with a cargo of plaster, the schooner *H. C. Higginson* of Rockland, Maine, had drifted around Massachusetts Bay all day Sunday until finally dashing against the rocks at the base of Atlantic Hill around 8 p.m. Mate E. C. Rood explained that the crew "stayed about the deck as long as we could. When we went aloft the captain was near the wheel, and refused to go into the rigging with us, as did one of the sailors, a native of Denmark. They were soon washed overboard by the sea and lost." Six members of the crew climbed skyward, all but one surviving to see the lifesavers arrive. "L. Brems, the steward, a resident of East Boston, was with us," said Rood, "but was unable to withstand the force of the gale, and at 2 a.m. he died in our arms and we lashed him to the mast."

As James and his men repaired their surfboat, Captain James Anderson of the Humane Society's volunteer crew at Crescent Beach in Cohasset and Keeper George H. Brown of the Life-Saving Service's North Scituate station had arrived and begun preparing their own crews for the rescue of the five men remaining alive aboard the *H. C.*

Higginson. Keeper Brown and his crew had slogged through nearly nine miles of mud and slush, all the while towing their beach apparatus cart, to reach the wreck, now submerged, decks awash, between two rocky ledges. The Keeper fired his Lyle gun, landing a line across the flying jibstay. The projectile from Captain Anderson's Hunt gun then boomed out of the cannon's mouth and soared straight and true toward its destination, closer to the stranded mariners. For a moment, it seemed as if the crew would be saved by breeches buoy, as the sailors worked quickly to make the hawser fast and secure the whipline, but wreckage floating in the water between the ship and the shore fouled the lines, making it impossible for the men to rig the breeches buoy apparatus and employ it. Three Humane Society volunteers from Cohasset took to a small, eleven-foot dory, against the better judgment of all ashore, and "rowed out through the roaring breakers at the imminent peril of their lives." They tried, unsuccessfully, to free the line, and returned to shore.

When the three young men returned, James and his crew were ready to make the next attempt. "The surf boat crew decided that if a dory could live in that sea then the best surf boat ever built in the country certainly ought to," stated the *Hingham Journal*, "and they quickly manned their noble craft and started on their third perilous trip of the day." James described the scene more matter-of-factly, saying, "As soon as the boat was repaired I launched and went off to save the men who could be seen in the rigging. The sea alongside of the vessel was terrible."

"The sea had gained in fury," wrote Kimball, "if such a thing were possible, the immense ridges of foam-crested surf bristling before them and advancing upon rank like a phalanx to meet them, seemed unconquerable, and there was scarcely a hope that they would be able to reach the wreck, if indeed they themselves escaped alive."

With waves cresting above the tops of the schooner's masts, the lifesavers pulled on their oars, while ashore "many a hardy mariner shook his head and said 'they can't do it.'" After what seemed an eternity to the overstrained shoulders and backs of the lifesavers, *Nantasket* reached the stern of the *H. C. Higginson*. As they pulled alongside the mizzenmast, the lifesavers watched as a man crawled out from beneath a furled sail and made his way from the mizzentop to the shrouds below, placing himself in position to receive a heaving line from James and leap into the sea. The other four men, in the foretop, were in no condition to undertake such a daring feat.

With the wind abating, James and his men now fought only the heavy running seas, driving their way forward along the schooner's side, yet it alone proved to be a formidable enough foe. As soon as they would make a few feet of progress, a large wave would propel them backwards again. For an hour they bent over their oars until achieving and maintaining a station alongside the mainmast, no mean feat, as "great care had to be exercised to prevent the boat from being dashed against the vessel and crushed." The men in the rigging had been clinging to both rope and life for fourteen hours, and now had to make their way from the fore to the maintop, as the lifesavers could pull no farther forward.

Their joints stiffened by the inactivity and the cold, the remaining crewmembers of the *H. C. Higginson* reached out for the hawser affixed to the foremast from the shot fired by Captain Anderson. One by one they began to descend to the main rigging. "It appeared every moment as if the swaying form would lose its hold and be swept away by the hungry waves which seemed to be leaping and stretching upward to seize him and plunge him into the sea below." James tossed a heaving line aboard, which a survivor tied fast around his waist. Putting his life, literally, into the tired but strong hands of the Humane Society volunteers, he leapt into the water and allowed the lifesavers to pull him into the *Nantasket*. The rest soon followed. The lifesavers then rowed for shore, with the body of the dead steward bound to the foretopmast ominously overlooking them all, an awful reminder of the unrelenting power of the sea and storm. It remained in position for another twenty-four hours before conditions allowed for its removal.

The lifesavers returned to raucous cheering on the beach, and were helped from their seats in the *Nantasket*. Hotelier and Hull selectman David O. Wade had wagons waiting to transport the "half-starved, half-frozen, more dead than alive men" to his home on Hull Street, where a local doctor awaited their arrival. One survivor from the *H. C. Higginson*, Alexander McQuarrie of Boston, announced that this was his second shipwreck within a year's time.

For the lifesavers, it was the fourth shipwreck to which they had been called in two days, but not the last. The three-masted schooner *Mattie E. Eaton* sat high and dry about 1000 feet away on the beach. By the time James and his men reached her, she was abandoned. Captain J. C. Gamage of Thomaston, Maine, later reported that he, his crew and a passenger had made it around Race Point and were southeast of Truro's Highland Lighthouse when the storm struck with terrific force, tearing away the foretopmast, jibboom and flying jibboom. The captain ran for Massachusetts Bay and Boston Harbor, hoping to ride out the storm at anchor near Minot's Light off Cohasset and Scituate, but the anchors dragged and the ship came ashore. As acted out elsewhere along the shore during the storm, the men climbed to the rigging at 1 a.m., and stayed there until the storm waters receded seven hours later. They then took to a lifeboat and rowed themselves to safety.

As the Humane Society's men returned from the *H.C. Higginson*, Keeper Brown and his surfmen from the North Scituate Life-saving Station reacted to the sighting of a British brig, *Alice*, coming ashore to the north along the beach. They fired a shot with their Lyle gun, which landed within what should have been easy reach of any sailor aboard, but no response was garnered, as heavy rain continued to hinder visibility. The Hull volunteers stopped to inquire about the *Alice*, and finding that no one could ascertain whether or not the crew was even alive, they launched *Nantasket* one more time. A half an hour's row to the brig revealed that the vessel, like the *Mattie E. Eaton*, had been abandoned. It had, in fact, parted its mooring at Gloucester, northwards across Boston Harbor, and drifted its way ashore at Nantasket Beach.

The lifesavers then retreated for home. They took time to refresh themselves, finally partaking of a meal as they watched the storm retreat. James returned to the area of Nantasket Beach late that evening to find that two men had taken a dory to the *Alice* and promptly lost their small craft to the sea. One of the men had made his way ashore, but the other remained aboard, and fearful that he might not survive the night aboard the brig, James rounded up one last volunteer crew and rowed to his rescue.

From sunrise on Sunday, November 25 to sundown on Monday, November 26, 62-year-old Joshua James had led 28 volunteer lifesavers from the Humane Society of the Commonwealth of Massachusetts to the rescue of 29 men on five different shipwrecks, using three different rescue boats and the breeches buoy.

There would be lifesaving medals, testimonials in their honor and even offers of money for James and his men, but no thoughts of such potential resulting rewards crossed their minds at the height of the storm, when lives were at stake. Instead, the volunteer lifesavers of Hull would always live by the creed so well stated by Francis James, a nephew of Joshua, and, of course, a volunteer lifesaver himself: "I'd like to think that if I was the one that was out there, someone would come for me."

The U.S. Life-Saving Service would soon be in town, but the local lifesavers had no intention of standing down when they arrived. Not even the Great Storm of 1888, as it soon came to be known, could break the will of the Humane Society's volunteers to carry out their mission to risk their own lives to save those sailors who became imperiled on the neighboring seas.

Chapter 1:
It Took a Blind Man to See

It took a blind man to see the need for the formation of the
Humane Society of the Commonwealth of Massachusetts.

Dr. Henry Moyes, Scotland-born and educated, blinded by
the ravages of smallpox at the age of three, arrived in the newly-
liberated United States of America in 1784. His objective in touring
the States was singular in its purpose. A failed lecturer on the theory
of music in his homeland, he crossed the Atlantic armed with a topic
that had generated interest enough in the Old World to convince his
friends to encourage him to make his first American speaking tour:
chemistry.

> Moyes landed in Boston in May 1784 and made the
> town his headquarters for his projected lecture tour.
> His educational invasion had begun. The new republic
> accepted Moyes with open arms; indeed, he must have
> been the first lecturer to cross the Atlantic for many
> years. A course quickly started in Boston ran to a
> successful conclusion. Culture-starved Bostonians were
> quick to respond to this popular form of adult
> education and pressed Moyes to deliver another
> course in the town. But he had planned the tour
> carefully and had drawn up a schedule of lectures
> which he meant to keep. The Bostonians were firmly,

1

but politely, told to wait. (John Anthony Harrison, "Blind Henry Moyes, 'An Excellent Lecturer in Philosophy.'" *Annals of Science*, Volume 13, Number 2, June 1957, pp. 109-125)

Moyes arrived in a United States that was cash poor, just four months removed from Congressional ratification of the Treaty of Paris, signifying the end of the revolution that founded the country. After eight years of war with Britain, the country had accumulated a national debt of $70,000,000. And although England was no longer formally at war with the new nation, it was encouraging others to carry on the battle. At the urging of England, Algiers declared war on the U.S. in 1785, impressing American sailors and waging a naval offensive on the country's merchant vessels. England, though, also quickly understood that it had reasons to once again be economically invested in its former colony. The first bales of American cotton to reach Great Britain did so in 1784.

As Moyes toured Philadelphia, Baltimore and Princeton in 1785, the United States showed signs of growth. The Continental Congress met in New York City on January 11 under President of the United States in Congress Assembled Richard Henry Lee. On January 27, the University of Georgia became the first state-chartered university in the country. Benjamin Franklin, recently returned from a stint as ambassador to France, during which he unsuccessfully tried to convince the French to take advantage of the concept of daylight savings time, announced his invention of bifocals in May. On July 6, Congress resolved unanimously that "the money unit of the United States be one dollar." By that time, the young nation had already turned its eyes toward westward expansion, as on May 20 Congress had passed the Land Ordinance of 1785, a planning tool for the division and sale of lands beyond the borders of the current recognized settlements hugging the Atlantic Coast.

Through this world Moyes traveled, lecturing to hundreds of interested listeners on topics such as "Heat," "Air," and "Vegetable Substances." When he finally returned to Boston in November 1785 to deliver his promised second course of lectures, Moyes wrote to a friend, Dr. Alexander Johnson, in England, saying "America is making rapid progress towards perfection, both in the road of politics and in the line of literature. The political body has already acquired particular strength and there are twelve universities now established in different parts of the federal union."

During his second tour of Boston, Moyes took advantage of a quiet winter's evening to share his thoughts with a small gathering on the 1774 formation in his home country of the "Humane Society for the recovery of persons apparently drowned," known by 1776 as simply the

Artist John Kay rendered this drawing of the blind physician Henry Moyes in 1796.

"Humane Society." Although not known to be an official agent of that organization, Moyes nevertheless ardently supported their efforts. While in the States, he received letters from his friend Dr. Johnson, regular updates on the society's investigations into medical processes through which it was hoped to restore life to the recently departed by drowning, suffocation or asphyxiation. "I am in hopes," Moyes wrote to Johnson, "that a humane society be established in the town of Boston; and I have reason to expect that, in the course of the ensuing winter, similar institutions will also be planted in New York and Philadelphia."

Boston responded quickly to Moyes' suggestion. On the night after the discussion with the doctor, one of his three guests – Reverend James Freeman, Dr. Aaron Dexter, or Royall Tyler, Esq. - procured a copy of the regulations of the Royal Humane Society from somewhere within the city of 18,000 citizens. The Rev. Freeman then transcribed them, with agreed upon changes, and handed copies to the others for the purposes of raising subscriptions throughout the city for the purposes of forming a similar institution. One man, Dr. Benjamin Waterhouse, who had previously been in correspondence with Dr. William Hawes, one of the founders of the Royal Humane Society, offered to carry a copy directly to the Governor of Massachusetts, James Bowdoin. "The Governor," reports Harrison, "already knew something of Moyes, as he had attended his recent lectures and had described them in a letter to his sister."

The enthusiasm initiated by the casual meeting with Dr. Moyes engendered strong support. On January 5, 1786, the subscribers met in a tavern at the corner of King Street and Mackerel Lane (today's State and Kilby Streets) to discuss the formal formation of an organization similar to the Royal Humane Society. The Bunch of Grapes Tavern was already an historic landmark in the city, the site of the founding of the first Masonic Lodge in North America in 1733, the feting of General George Washington after the extirpation of the British from Boston in 1775, and a bonfire composed of Royal arms pulled from buildings around the city after the reading of the Declaration of Independence in 1776.

> On a certain fair day, or it may have been night, in 1785 (sic), there was born in the old inn, not a babe, but a project, which must by no means be forgotten, for it had as sponsors James Bowdoin, Rev. James Freeman, and other noted men, and was destined to make a little stir in the world. Let there be no regret that it was not a veritable flesh-and-blood babe, for no human suckling known to our annals ever grew up to

be such a power for good in the community as the Boston Humane Society.

Few among its careless beneficiaries of the present day know or care that this same Humane Society, organized by those half dozen men over Landlord Coleman's good madeira, was instrumental in founding our first asylums for the insane and for lying-in women, our first free beds in hospitals, our lifeboats, huts for shelter, and all the life-saving gear on our rugged seacoast. (Edwin Lassetter Bynner, "The Old Bunch of Grapes Tavern," *The Atlantic Monthly*, Vol. LXIV, December 1889, No. CCCLXXXVI, p. 732.)

Dr. Moyes had left Boston by the time of the meeting, announcing his next round of lectures in Philadelphia on December 30, 1785. The blind doctor sailed for England from Charleston that May, leaving the future of the study of the restoration of the "apparently drowned" in America in the hands of the people of Boston, Philadelphia and New York.

The idea, an organization driven by the desire to foster study and practice of methods of saving lives, particularly drowning victims, was manifested through a series of rules and regulations drawn up at the tavern that day in 1786. The organization's governing hierarchical structure, twelve trustees, among whom would serve a president, two vice presidents, a recording secretary, a corresponding secretary and a treasurer, was also established that day. With James Bowdoin as the first president, "The Institution of the Humane Society of the Commonwealth of Massachusetts" presented its case to the people of Boston through the printing of its mission and regulations:

From a variety of faithful experiments, and incontestable facts, it is now considered as an established truth, that the total suspension of the vital functions of the animal body is by no means incompatible with life; and consequently, the marks of apparent death may subsist without any necessary implication of an absolute extinction of the animating principle.

The boundary line between life and death, or the distinguishing signs of the latter, are objects to which the utmost efforts of the human capacity have never yet attained. Nor can we, with any degree of certainty, pronounce, that an animal is dead, until the most unequivocal proofs of putrefaction have been furnished.

From these facts it might reasonably be expected, that were proper measures to be adopted, especially in cases peculiarly doubtful, we might frequently be enabled to restore to full life, and the enjoyment of it, a beloved friend, or a valuable member of society. And indeed, numerous successful instances might be adduced in the cases of persons, who would in a few hours have been consigned to an untimely grave; and perhaps have suffered all the horrors of inevitable death, attended with a consciousness of their own terrible situation...

Upon these considerations, societies have been formed in various parts of Europe for promoting attempts to recover persons from apparent death, especially in cases of suffocation and drowning. The Humane Society established in Great-Britain, in 1774, has been very successful. Within ten years from its institution, out of 1300 persons apparently dead from drowning, 790 have been restored to their friends and country. Many of them, no doubt, useful and valuable men.

For an institution of this nature a considerable fund is necessary. A proper apparatus must be procured. And many occasional expences will unavoidably occur. The cause of humanity, however, deserves every encouragement. And to promote that cause, it is to be hoped the benevolent will liberally subscribe.

The wording of the original pamphlet corroborates the thoughts of DeWitt Clinton, future Governor of New York, then a student at Columbia University. The dark age of communication between the average citizens of the American colonies and their contemporaries in England during the revolution had kept the ten years' worth of research in the fields of natural history and chemistry a secret from those on the western side of the Atlantic. As such, according to Clinton, Moyes "had the merit of sowing the first seeds of this science in this country, redeemed from the follies of Alchemy, the visions of elixirs and transmutations, and founded on the experimental science of Bacon." The notion of retrieving life from the grasp of death probably seemed impossible to many Bostonians, but the members of the "Institution," as it was called, were willing to put their money on the line to defend their belief in the power of science, and their faith in the long list of success stories emanating from England.

Under rule VIII "for the regulation of a Society instituted in the town of Boston, for the recovery of persons who meet with such accidents as produce in them the appearance of death," the founders declared that when any such accident occurred, "the person who shall first discover, and endeavour to recover the subject, shall be entitled to receive from the Treasurer of the Society, a sum not exceeding forty-eight shillings, nor less than six shillings, lawful money, at the discretion of the Trustees." Rule IX offered no more than nine shillings to the person that first reported such accidents to one of the institution's physicians, and rule XIV promised no more than thirty shillings to one "who shall, by signal exertion, save another from death."

In a separate focus of the primary mission of the Humane Society, the founders declared that the Trustees would be responsible for securing the services of a public lecturer to speak on the second Tuesday of every June on "some medical subject connected with the principal objects of this Society." On that same day each year, the Society would "publicly adjudge a silver medal, not exceeding the value of one guinea, to the author of the most approved dissertation which they shall have received in the course of the preceding year, upon some medical subject connected with the principal objects of

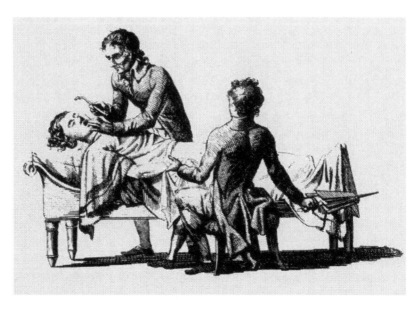

In its earliest days, the Humane Society focused its efforts on resuscitation and revival of the "apparently drowned."

this Society, and the Society shall order the same to be printed at their expence, provided it shall be agreeable to the author's inclination." From the outset, the founders saw the dissemination of medical knowledge as a crucial element of their exertions.

The original pamphlet, reprinted two years later, included a treatise on "Methods of Treatment to be used with Persons apparently dead from drowning," offering a nine-step course of action as proof of the possibilities presented by scientific study in Europe. The procedure called for the removal of obstructions from the mouth and the stripping away of wet clothing; "the smoke of tobacco thrown up the fundament"; and the rubbing of the skin. "The nostrils may be every now and then tickled with a feather; snuff and volatiles, should be occasionally made use of, to excite sneezing if possible," it continued.

> The methods which have been so fully recommended,
> are to be made use of with vigour for several hours,
> although no favourable circumstances should arise;

8

for it is a vulgar and dangerous opinion to suppose that persons are irrecoverable, because life does not soon make its appearance; and upon this opinion, an immense number of the seemingly dead have been committed to the grave; who might have been RESTORED TO LIFE by *resolution* and *perseverance* in the plans of treatment now recommended.

Seventy-eight subscribers lent their names to the pamphlet, among them the most important men of the city of Boston at the time. Doctors John Warren, Benjamin Waterhouse and Aaron Dexter founded Harvard Medical School in 1782. Warren had served under General Washington with the Continental Army as a surgeon during the American Revolution. Massachusetts Attorney General Robert Treat Paine served as a delegate to the Continental Congress and signed the Declaration of Independence. Oliver Wendell, Esq., was so well-thought of that the town of Wendell, Massachusetts, took its name from him in 1781, while he was still alive. Thomas Russell of Charlestown served as President of the Society for propagating the Gospel among Indians and others in North America, the Agricultural Society, the Society for the Advice of Immigrants, the Boston Chamber of Commerce and the National Bank in Boston.

"Such, in brief survey, was the group of Boston worthies to whom the fortunes of the Humane Society were first committed," writes Mark Anthony DeWolfe Howe in *The Humane Society of the Commonwealth of Massachusetts* in 1918. Furthermore,

To a conspicuous degree they represented the humanitarian, scientific, and public-spirited interests of their community. To what extent they were conscious of the possibilities of the undertaking which they launched, it is impossible at this time to declare with certainty. In all the printed expressions of their aims, however, there is a note of confident idealism, a sense of responsibility perhaps most truly characterized by the word 'religious,' which seems to speak for a simple, uncomplicated view of life and its value, marking the

n

Dr. John Warren, shown in this oil on canvas portrait by Rembrandt Peale now in the collection of the Harvard University Portrait Collection, characterized the founders of the Humane Society: selfless, compassionate, and concerned for his fellow man.

timent in a generous and intelligent community first standing squarely upon its own feet.

The birth of the Humane Society of the Commonwealth of Massachusetts was complete. But it existed then as merely the ethereal embodiment of good intention. No lives had yet been saved by its formation. No victim of apparent drowning had been rescued from death by the distribution of pamphlets. To truly test the validity and merit of the organization of the society, those good intentions would have to be put to practical use for the betterment of humanity.

Chapter 2:
A Small Step

There can be no doubt that a significant portion of the Boston community looked to the early missives from the Humane Society with disbelief, possibly even derision. The statement in the first pamphlet that declared "it is a vulgar and dangerous opinion to suppose that persons are irrecoverable, because life does not soon make its appearance" must have seemed, for some, utter folly. A leap of faith was called for by many to ensure the forward progress towards the new organization's goals and visions for resuscitation of life from the grip of death.

The pamphlet was a first, important step, but a more imperative plan of action soon arose. While printed dissertations on how to preserve life after perceived drowning, not to mention "hanging, convulsion, fits, cold, suffocation by damps, or noxious vapors, the confined air of wells, cisterns, caves, or the must of fermenting liquors," supplied the knowledge on how to save lives, supplying the tools to enact those rescues became of supreme significance to the society.

Prescribing heavily to the practice of blowing smoke into the intestines as a method of restoration, the society announced in a footnote to the "Methods of Treatment to be used with Persons apparently dead from drowning" that a number of fumigators for the purpose "will soon be procured, and notice will be given where they shall be deposited." By 1787, two sets had been purchased and deposited, one with Dr. John Warren on School Street, the other with Dr. David Townsend on Essex Street. By 1796, three more sets could be found throughout Boston.

The acquisition of the fumigators signaled the commencement of a period of stockpiling of reactive lifesaving equipment in the city, available to any citizen should an emergency arise, an idea that fundamentally extended to the seacoast that same year.

In 1787, the Humane Society placed three huts of refuge on exposed areas of Massachusetts coastline, a clear signal of the importance of maritime commerce to the people of the new state. The society erected the first three huts at significant points of danger along traditional coastwise trade routes. The first listed hut, at "Scituate Beach," sat a mile south of the Fourth Cliff headland on the Humarock peninsula. At that time, the North River flowed out at about the approximate location of today's Rexhame Beach, having turned south-southeast from inside Fourth Cliff and running alongside the peninsula for several miles. White's Ferry, the site of a ferryboat across the river from Marshfield to Humarock since 1638, ran across the river, and across the narrow peninsula at about that point rested the Humane Society hut. Shipbuilding had been carried on along the banks of the North River for about a hundred years to that point, and that industry was rapidly approaching what would turn out to be the most productive period in its history. Furthermore, the river served as a fishery, harvesting grounds for saltmarsh hay used for thatch and feed and sported several landing sites for transportation of farmed goods to outside markets. The passage along the Scituate and Marshfield coast also served as the trade route between Boston and Plymouth, the two largest communities in the region. A hut at the Scituate Beach site theoretically intercepted all of this traffic.

To the north, a second hut stood on the southern side of another, rocky headland in Hull. Point Allerton (sometimes referred to as "Alderton," yet nevertheless named for the Pilgrim Isaac Allerton) appeared as the first point of land for mariners traveling to Boston after crossing Cape Cod Bay. A lighted bowl of pitch or tar, America's first lighted aid to navigation, had stood on the bluff's apex in 1679, and the first American lighthouse, Boston Light, illuminated the

This 1775 map and chart of Boston Harbor showed the treacherousness of the approach to the city.

eponymous Lighthouse Channel for the first time in 1716 a mile across the water on Little Brewster Island. Point Allerton stands as the northernmost reach of the sandy Nantasket peninsula, a seven mile stretch of sand and rock standing in the way of access to the towns of Quincy Bay. Ships headed for Boston, Quincy, Weymouth or Hingham (Hull, or Nantasket, had a small population of about 125 residents in 1787, and was not a major mercantile port) that could not resist the power of northeast storms often stranded on the point, the three and a half miles of sandy Nantasket Beach, or worse, struck offshore ledges on the way there.

The third hut, placed on the west end of Lovell's Island, marked a halfway point for ships entering Boston Harbor. After clearing Point Allerton, entering Lighthouse Channel and passing the outer harbor islands named for Elder William Brewster of Pilgrim fame and steering clear of a long, sandy spit coming off the largest of those islands, ships entered the Narrows, the northwesterly passage between Gallops, George's and Lovell's islands. The western shore of the island marked the eastern side of the inbound and outbound passages. More importantly, the citing of the hut on that spot placed it centrally between the three islands, allowing notionally easy access for sailors wrecked on any one of them.

In 1789, the Humane Society constructed three more such huts, on the eastern side of Lovell's Island, on the southwest end of "Calef" or Calf Island and on Nantasket Beach across from Strawberry Hill, about halfway down the Hull peninsula, on what was at that time a barren, open piece of land between Hull Village and a settlement at the Hull-Hingham-Cohasset boundary. John Avery, Jr., recording secretary for the society, submitted an announcement to the *Columbian Centinel* that ran on October 16, 1790, stating that the Society had built the huts, and "have caused poles to be erected with balls painted white to point out where said Houses stand, and have repeatedly deposited in them, the necessary means of kindling and preserving a fire, and some other means necessary for the comfort and relief of the Ship-wrecked Mariner."

The first six huts of refuge cost the society a total of $215, allocated from the subscriber's donations. They gave a stranded sailor a fighting chance where he had never had one before, a place to hide from the fury of a storm and indeed to stay warm until it spent its energy. The smoke from the fireplace would alert locals within spotting scope distance of the presence of, perhaps, someone in need.

Just who burned the wood provided, though, sometimes had to be called into question. The abuse of these early shelters became an unfortunate and recurring theme. An institutional history published by the Trustees in 1845 stated that, "Scarcely had one been erected on Lovell's Island, in 1789, before it was found necessary to offer rewards for the discovery of the perpetrators of so base an outrage." Avery's announcement in the *Columbian Centinel*, fell short of an offer for a reward, but went on to say that the Trustees of the Humane Society

> ...wish that the benevolent purpose for which the said
> Huts have been erected and the eminent service they
> have already been to several Persons, may protect

them from lawless depredations; and whereas said Houses are frequently robbed of the means necessary for the relief aforesaid by Persons destitute of the feelings of humanity, the Trustees request those who reside in the vicinity of the said Huts to use their utmost care that the articles deposited therein may remain uninjured.

An anonymous writer narrated a tale of two shipwrecked sailors in Hull in November 1794, in a letter published in the *Columbian Centinel* on April 11, 1795. A ship sailing from Cape Ann had driven ashore on the point, and its two sailors "with much difficulty swam, or otherwise got on shore; when, arrived at the asylum erected by humanity, they were disappointed of relief, the tinder box being wet, and otherwise in a situation useless to them; the provisions devoured by the mice, or some inhuman mouse in the shape of a man." The two men, cold and stunned from their unfortunate accident, stumbled out onto the beach, unknowing of where to turn for help. By chance, they encountered a duck hunter preparing for the day's shoot on the plains of the peninsula, and he led them to safe lodging well down the beach. The anonymous "Well Wisher" suggested that paid guardians be hired to watch over the buildings, especially during times of inclement weather. This arrangement would eventually come to pass, with the creation of professionally staffed lifeboat stations operated by the United States Life-Saving Service, but that accomplishment loomed foggily decades into the future.

Slowly, though, that foggy future began to reveal itself. On December 15, 1802, the brigantine *Elizabeth*, headed or Boston, had taken on a pilot in Lighthouse Channel, but was unable to advance as, already in bad condition, the ship faced a growing northwest wind. At 2 a.m. on the 16th, her anchor chains let go, and twelve hours later the wind dashed the vessel against the Point Allerton Bar. Four young mates dove overboard and swam fifty yards for shore, hoping to head for the local village. One gave up on the way, giving out physically, but thanks to information from the other three, the locals went to his aid. At 4 p.m., with the storm still raging, the pilot Thomas Knox tied a rope around himself, securing the other end to the rest of the people aboard. He swam to the shore and then turned and pulled the rest onto the beach behind him. They headed for the safety of the Humane Society hut of refuge, but "who can describe their extreme grief and disappointment, when, upon their arrival, they found no fire works, candles or straw, and but a small quantity of wood!"

The same situation had arisen as before, but in this case, a new wrinkle turned the story from one of near-total disaster to complete salvation. The people of Hull braved the storm with armloads of combustible material, forcing their way through the wind to deliver the goods to the hut to start a proper, life-preserving fire. All of the sailors survived. The event presaged the recruiting local volunteers to be active participants in the Society's life-saving efforts, rather than just sentinels overseeing the security of the huts.

Still, Reverend Dr. John Lathrop and Reverend Samuel Parker, tasked with reviewing the case for the Trustees, stated

> ...it is with great regret that your committee observe, that there are found in a civilized country, persons so abandoned and devoid of every principle of humanity, as to take from those houses, erected from principles of benevolence, to alleviate the distresses of the unfortunate shipwrecked seamen, the tinderbox, candles, straw and fuel, with which they are supplied every year by this society, as was the case with this to which these persons resorted; and thereby leave these distressed people to perish for want of articles of so small value, as not to be an object worth purloining. Such inhumanity is a disgrace to any people, that are not barbarians.

The question may well be asked, and certainly was, and repeatedly, as to who the hut of refuge bandits were. Several groups of people stood as obvious suspects. Duck hunters, like the compassionate one that saved the men from the Cape Ann schooner, roamed the plains of Hull well prior to sunrise, before most of the townspeople of Hull might have any reason to venture out onto the distant beach behind the headland. And they used similar small, hunting shanties that mimicked the huts on a regular basis. Second, the possibility exists that victims of small shipwrecks, completely unknown to the local residents, and who migrated southwards along the beach away from the village at Hull, may have used the firewood to good purpose. Third, though, the real possibility existed that thieves, most likely from the local populace, looted the huts. These problems could be exacerbated on offshore islands, or even more remote stations, like on the outer beach of Cape Cod, where even less vigilance could be practiced.

The 1845 *History of the Humane Society of Massachusetts* noted that "even to the present, in instances not a few, have the Trustees found themselves obliged to repair the wastes of this peculiarly cruel and wanton depredation..."

Naturalist, transcendentalist and author Henry David Thoreau encountered more than one Humane Society hut of refuge during one of his three trips to Cape Cod in the 1850s, recounted in his posthumously published book by that name. Walking the beach, Thoreau and a friend "came to a Charity-house, which we looked into to see how the shipwrecked mariner might fare." The building "had neither window, nor sliding shutter, nor clapboards, nor paint...there was a rusty nail put through the staple." One at a time, he and his friend peered into the building through a knothole in the door, "not knowing how many shipwrecked men's bones we might see at last."

Short of that, "a chimney rushed red on our sight...there were some stones and some loose wood on the floor, and an empty fireplace at the further end, but it was not supplied with matches, or straw, or hay, that we could see...Indeed, it was the wreck of all cosmical beauty there within."

Thoreau, the eternal pessimist, followed these words with a scathing report.

> This then, is what charity hides! Virtues antique and far away with ever a rusty nail over the latch; and very difficult to keep in repair, withal, it is so uncertain whether any will ever gain the beach near you. So we shivered round about, not being able to get into it,

Concord's Henry David Thoreau was one of the first detractors of the work of the Humane Society, as so described in his posthumously published book Cape Cod.

ever and anon looking through the knot-hole into that night without a star, until we concluded that it was not a *humane* house at all, but a sea-side box, now shut up, belonging to some of the family of Night or Chaos, where they spent their summers by the sea, for the sake of the sea-breeze, and that it was not proper for us to be prying into their concerns.

Still, another of Thoreau's descriptions of the houses may be as accurate a picture as modern readers are ever to get: "The gull flew around and screamed over them; the roar of the ocean in storms, and the lapse of waves in calms, alone resounds through them, all dark and empty within, year in, year out, except, perchance on one memorable night."

To this day, the Massachusetts General Laws include one specifically targeted at the preservation of the huts of refuge and their contents, M.G.L. Chapter 266: Section 133: "Humane society; injury to property."

> Whoever unlawfully enters a house, boat house or hut which is the property of the Humane Society of the Commonwealth of Massachusetts and willfully injures, removes or carries away any property belonging to said society, or willfully injures or unlawfully uses or commits any trespass upon the property of said society which is intended or kept for the purpose of saving or preserving human life, or commits any trespass upon such house, hut or boat house, shall be punished by a fine of not more than two hundred dollars or by imprisonment for not more than six months; but the penalties of this section shall not apply to persons for whose use said boats, houses and other property are intended and kept. Pilots, sheriffs and their deputies, and constables shall make complaint against all persons guilty of a violation of this section. One half of any fine paid hereunder shall be paid to the person who gives information upon which a conviction is obtained.

The Humane Society's huts of refuge marked a small, stumbling step in the proper direction towards the humanitarian ideal of man caring for man, but it was at least a step.

Chapter 3:
Rapid Growth

By 1790, the Humane Society of the Commonwealth of Massachusetts had established itself as the premier organization in its field in the United States, and as one of few existing at that time in the world. In China, the Chinkiang Association for Saving Life had been in operation on the Yangtze River since at least 1708, if not before that date. Holland's Institution for the Recovery of Drowned Persons dated from 1767 and the Royal Humane Society, the organization off which the Massachusetts body had been patterned, formed in 1774.

Almost immediately after the initial gathering of interested souls at the Bunch of Grapes Tavern in January 1786, the Society began granting cash rewards to those folks who by a "signal exertion" saved the lives of their fellow humans. That year, the Society gave twenty-eight shillings to young Andrew Sloane for pulling a boy who had fallen into a mill pond (near today's Causeway Street) to a place of safety, where he could be properly restored, the first such pecuniary reward. Similar disbursements took place in the years to come.

In July 1789 the Society awarded its first gold medal to a Lieutenant Scott, Royal Navy. According to all accounts extant, Scott leapt from the stern of the *Leopard* and into Boston Harbor to save a drowning boy. (The 4th rate, 50-gun ship *Leopard*, famous for its confrontation with the American frigate *Chesapeake* in 1807, was not launched until 1790. Most historical sources list a gap between the decommissioning of the 4th rate *Leopard* constructed in 1741 (which served until 1761) and the famous ship. Only one source, Patrick Boniface's *Cats and Cathedrals*, lists another vessel in between the 1741 and 1790 *Leopards*, built in 1782. Lt. Scott, whose first name has not come down through history, apparently served on the 1782-built 4th rate ship.) No more details currently exist as to the act of bravery.

By this time, the society itself had begun collecting accolades of its own. On June 22, 1788, General George Washington wrote and sent a letter to Reverend Dr. John Lathrop, stating,

> I observe, with singular satisfaction, the cases in which your benevolent institution has been instrumental in recalling some of our fellow creatures (as it were) from beyond the gates of eternity, and has given occasion for the hearts of parents and friends to leap for joy. The provision made for shipwrecked mariners is also highly estimable in the view of every philanthropic mind and greatly consolatory to that suffering part of the community. These things will draw upon you the blessings of those who were ready to perish. These works of charity and good-will towards men reflect, in my estimation, great luster upon the authors, and presage an era of still farther improvements. How pitiful, in the eye of reason and religion, is that false ambition which desolates the world with fire and sword for the purposes of conquest and fame; when compared to the milder virtues of making our neighbors and our fellow men as happy as their frail conditions and perishable natures will permit them to be!

Two and a half years later, the young Society incorporated as a public charity under Massachusetts law, on February 23, 1791, signed by Governor John Hancock. The text of the act "To Incorporate and Establish a Society by the name of The Humane Society of the

Commonwealth of Massachusetts" gave its purpose as "the recovery of persons who meet with such accidents in them the appearance of death, and for promoting the cause of humanity, by pursuing such means from time to time, as shall have for their object the preservation of human life, and the alleviation of its miseries." The phrase "promoting the cause of humanity" provided for a wide interpretation of the Society's future missions, a factor that would certainly come into play as the years went by. More importantly for the moment, the incorporation meant that the society could accept donations of cash, goods or land and use them for the purposes stated in the act.

More praise and support for the Society's work came through international channels. In response to an act of bravery on the part of Frenchman Julien Jean Durotior, that being his rescue of two shipwrecked sailors near Nantucket Shoals in December 1790, the Society had awarded a gold medal. The French National Assembly responded with a humble letter of thanks and appreciation. Grenot Vaublanc, President of the assembly, congratulated the Society for its initiatives, saying "The whole world will be solicitous to pay a just homage to the benevolent citizens, whom, impelled by the generous ardour of rendering themselves useful to their fellow men, have formed an association under the sublime title of the Humane Society of Massachusetts – instituted to relieve the unfortunate, and to reward those who imitate its noble intention." Furthermore, reflective of the sincerest form of flattery, Vaublanc noted that the assembly had voted to "form one philanthropic society, which will keep up with that of Massachusetts, a happy intercourse of virtues and fraternal regard, which no other interests will ever be able to interrupt." Embroiled in a near constant state of turmoil as the nation sought to determine its governing structure, France would be in an undeclared war with the United States by the end of the decade.

As 1800 approached, the Society continued to make important gains in achieving its mission. They awarded their third gold medal in 1793, to a man who rescued the crew of a wrecked ship on Duxbury Beach. They awarded four silver medals, extended the thanks of the society three times (including once to Governor Hancock in response to the approval of the act of incorporation) and paid out 147 financial rewards for acts of "signal exertion."

Unfortunately, though, as with the placement of the houses of refuge, the awards system came with problems brought on by the darker side of human nature. By 1799, the Society realized that certain citizens had overly dramatized the roles they had played in rescues deemed worthy of financial rewards. That year the Society amended its definition of its signature phrase.

> By a signal exertion the Trustees conceive must be understood something more than barely reaching out the hand, or throwing a rope from a wharf, or a boat, or even wading into the water to help a man's depth, and rescuing a man from drowning; for the principles of common humanity and sympathy are sufficient motives for such exertions; but it must include the endangering of his own life, or incurring some damage, by impairing the health, or injuring his apparel or other property. In any or all these cases the Trustees are ready to grant adequate reward, when properly authenticated, but do not think themselves warranted by the regulations of the society to bestow them in other cases.

Much like the problem with vandalism and robbery at the huts of refuge, attempts to creatively relieve the Society of its funds would continue to be a problem throughout its early existence. During the 1826 annual meeting, Trustee John Heard, Jr., commented that he believed that "several persons represented to have been saved from drowning, had intentionally thrown themselves into the Mill Creek, for the purpose of obtaining the Society's premiums." As much as it tried to save humanity, the Humane Society had to fight it.

Toward that end, such difficulties simply served to frustrate the Trustees temporarily, whenever they flared up. Ultimately, the Society would always press forward with its goals of finding new ways to achieve its ends. The dawn of the nineteenth century promised a landmark moment for the Society, one that would set the organization down a road toward eternal recognition as the foremost shore-based lifesaving organization for mariners in distress at sea in the United States, and the basis upon which America's national search and rescue system has since been built.

—

Chapter 4:
Action

For the first decade of its existence, the Humane Society established itself as a reactive lifesaving organization. Huts of refuge were best utilized only once the shipwrecked had come ashore; fumigators could revive the apparently drowned only after they had succumbed to the consequences of their predicaments. If anything, though, the first decade also showed that the organization was a progressive one, willing to try new ideas if they promised to be of potential benefit to humanity. As the century turned, the Trustees began examining a way to turn the Society from a reactive organization to a proactive one.

On November 2, 1801, the Trustees listened to the reading of a letter sent to them from Dr. William Hawes, treasurer of the Royal Humane Society in London, regarding the construction of a "life-boat" in South Shields, a shipbuilding town at the mouth of the Tyne River, north of London. "To our great satisfaction," Hawes reported, "she has been the means of saving the lives of many of our fellow creatures, who could by no other means have been preserved."

Hawes described the boat as thirty feet long and ten feet wide, "in form much resembling a common Greenland boat, except the bottom, which is much flatter." Heavily laden with buoyant cork, the boat sat ten men, double-banked, with steering oars at either end. "Long poles are provided for the men, to keep the boat from being drove broad-side to the shore either in going off or landing." Light of draft, the boat could hold up to twenty people.

The Englishman's description of the boat became more dramatic. "The boat is able to contend with the most tremendous sea, and broken water," he wrote, "and never, in any one instance, has she failed in bringing the crew in distress into safety." The men who rowed the lifeboat, he claimed, scoffed at the cork lifejackets provided for them, believing that the boat would never put them in a position to use them.

"She has surprised every nautical man that has seen her contend with the waves," Hawes testified.

The notion of dedicating boats for exclusive use in saving lives – and property - had arisen during the eighteenth century in several places around the globe. The Chinese, again, were ahead of the curve, using a variety of watercraft as early as 1737 along the Yangtze River. The Dutch considered the construction of lifesaving-specific boats in 1769, although it is uncertain whether or not they were ever built. Liverpool residents used whaleboats and other small vessels for exclusive lifesaving use in 1776.

British coachbuilder Lionel Lukin began experimenting with what he would later call an "unimmergible" boat in the 1780s, hoping simply to improve upon the design of a Norway yawl by adding cork for flotation and an iron keel for stability. When, in 1785, he began to understand the potential value of his boat to the burgeoning world of coastal lifesaving, he applied for and received a patent for his design. The following year, at the request of Dr. John Sharpe of the Bishop Crewe Charitable Trust in Bamburgh, Lukin converted a Northumberland coble, an open-decked boat used primarily for fishing on the northeast coast of England, to an "unimmergible" lifeboat. No records exist of the boat being used for lifesaving purposes, but the concept of a lifeboat, nonetheless, had reached the English-speaking world.

WILLIAM HAWES MD

Dr. William Hawes, founder of the Royal Humane Society, reported on the construction of a "life-boat" in London, creating a new wave of excitement in Boston over the potential of life-saving operations.

As with many advances in the technology and methodology of coastal lifesaving through the centuries, the call for a purpose-built lifeboat came as a result of a tragedy. Hundreds of onlookers stood by helplessly on March 5, 1789, as the collier *Adventure* ran into trouble off the mouth of the Tyne. Just a few hundred yards from shore, the ship broke to pieces and one by one the sailors drowned before the eyes of the people on shore until all had perished. A group of prominent local businessmen, later known as the "Gentlemen of the Lawe House," watching from their meeting house atop a bluff, determined that such an event should not have to occur again, and immediately initiated a contest for the a new lifeboat design. Lukin entered, and lost.

The winning design, by inventor and late Renaissance man William Wouldhave, of North Shields, pioneered the concept of self-righting capability (Lukin and Wouldhave supporters still argue which man was the true inventor of the lifeboat). The Gentlemen of the Lawe House charged Henry Greathead of South Shields, who had entered a design and lost, to take the best elements of all the designs submitted and build a lifeboat to be used by the lifesavers of the newly-formed Tynemouth Humane Society. Greathead called his first lifeboat *Original*, and Hawes' letter spoke of this specific design

Lifeboat designer Henry Greathead of South Shields, at the mouth of the Tyne River, designed the lifeboat Original, *from which Humane Society lifeboat proponents drew inspiration.*

(Greathead built forty-four more lifeboats on this pattern between 1790 and 1810).

On June 14, 1803, John Sylvester John Gardiner, Assistant Minister of the Trinity Church, delivered a sermon at the semiannual meeting of the Humane Society of the Commonwealth of Massachusetts. "It may not, Gentlemen," he orated,

> ...be impertinent to the subject of this discourse, and to the occasion of our present meeting, to remark on a late invention, which appears to be highly useful, in the preservation of human life.
>
> The invention I mean is the Life-boat, the honour of which is due to Mr. Greathead, a boat-builder, at Shields, in England; for which he has received, independent of small gratuities from private societies, one hundred pounds sterling from Trinity House, and a grant of twelve hundred from the British Parliament. This boat contains thirty persons with ease, can neither sink nor overset, and rides, with perfect security, where no other floating machine could exist. The price of a ten-oared boat, which is the largest, amounts to one hundred and sixty pounds sterling.

Gardiner continued his sermon by describing the elements of the boat from his admittedly non-technical point of view. He recounted how Greathead told a committee of the House of Commons of his inspiration for a high bow and stern and a curved keel. Cut a sphere into quarters, Greathead said, and submerge one piece in water. "This thrown into the sea, or broken water, cannot be upset, or lie with the bottom upwards."

Gardiner then made his pitch.

> Would it not be advisable, to procure a model of this boat, with an accurate description of its capabilities? If the expense should be found too great for ships to furnish themselves with it, or even for private societies to supply, could not the humanity of the Legislature be excited to raise a tax for this purpose? A few boats of this kind, distributed along the coast, and stationed at places, where shipwreck is most common, might be the means, of saving, in the course of time, thousands of valuable lives to their country and friends. I mean not however, to obtrude, but to offer my sentiments on this subject, leaving it to your superior judgment, Mr. President, and Gentlemen of this society, to consider the propriety of the application.

Three years later, as an appendix to the 1806 published discourse of Reverend Thaddeus Mason Harris, an anonymous member of the Society delivered a six-page poem entitled simply "The Life Boat," excerpted here:

> Let now, *Humanity*, like gifts display
> Along the shores of *Massachusetts Bay*;
> Exult when *Greathead's* blest invention saves,
> While breaks the *Londoner* – or roar the *Graves*,
> Where *Great Nahant* uprears his sea wreath'd head,
> Or bays of *Ipswich* broader basons spread,
> Or where *Plumb Island* hears the frequent voice

John Sylvester John Gardiner delivered a sermon in Boston in 1803 that opened the eyes of the Society to the potential of lifeboat rescues of mariners in distress at sea. (Courtesy of Ian Gardiner).

Of shipwreck'd seamen – be the better choice;
'Tis equal – unregarded be the Muse,
So may the pausing mind, judicious, choose.
Where *Scituate's* cliffs, mid elemental strife,
Lift their bold heads, preserve the sinking life;
Or where *Cohasset's* castled rocks emerge,
Redeem the victim from the whelming surge.

The Society's first action in regards to the construction or purchase of a lifeboat came the following year. Again, as an appendix to the annual discourse, this one delivered by Reverend William Emerson, the Society stated its intentions.

It has been one of the objects of the Humane Society to provide a life boat, which may prove the means of preserving many mariners coming upon our coasts in the seasons of storms. There is one now building at Nantucket, which will be finished in a few weeks, and exhibited in the harbour of Boston. It is not yet determined what part of the coasts is best to keep the boat the ensuing season, but generally thought it will be somewhere near the shores of Plymouth.

Financial records show that in 1807 the society paid out its single greatest expense to date, $1,433.11, as "Expenses of the Life Boat," with an additional $160 for "Shed at Cohasset." Cohasset, formerly a precinct of neighboring Hingham, was chiefly a town of seafarers, one that stood out for its treacherously rocky coastline. Offshore, several sunken ledges, just feet underwater at low tides, beckoned sailors to their doom. Mid-nineteenth century engineering would finally conquer the ledges through the construction of Minot's Lighthouse on one of them, but, prior to the arrival of the lifeboat, the best a sailor could hope for was to steer well clear of the ledges or, if blown near them by overpowering winds, to have the end come quickly.

The choice of Cohasset for the placement of the first lifeboat made sense from a practical standpoint. Coming down the coast from the northern end of the South Shore, Boston Light lit the entrance into the approach to Boston Harbor. One Humane Society hut of refuge stood just south of Point Allerton while another rose out of the sands of Nantasket Beach halfway down the peninsula. The lifeboat guarded the Cohasset coastline (Cohasset means "the long, rocky place" in Algonquian), while another hut of refuge guarded the sandy stretch of Humarock below Fourth Cliff in Scituate. Finally, the approach to Plymouth from the north, along the long, sandy stretch of Duxbury

Beach, received two huts of refuge in 1806. Where sloping, sandy beaches dominated the shoreline, huts of refuge had been deemed satisfactory for lifesaving purposes; where unyielding rock stood ready to claim ships and men, lifeboats would be preferred.

In 1810, the society apparently forewent the publication of the discourse of Reverend John Kirkland who, being busy with his newfound duties as President of Harvard, never found time to finish his revisions to his lecture. Instead, it printed the usual appendix, recounting the actions of the organization during the previous year. News of the lifeboat covered three pages.

> The life boat belonging to the Massachusetts Humane Society is stationed at Cohasset, under the immediate care and discretion of Captains John Lathrop and Peter Lathrop of that town. She measures thirty feet by ten; in form much resembles a common whale boat, except the bottom, which is much flatter; and is lined with cork inside and outside of the gunwale, about two feet in breadth, and the seats underneath, together with the stem and stern, are filled with cork also.

The fact that the boat resembled a whaleboat came as no mistake. The builder, William Raymond of Nantucket (Edward Stackpole's *Life Saving Nantucket* has him as Henry Raymond) built whaleboats for a living. Captain Gideon Gardner, a member of the Humane Society, and soon to be a U.S. representative, oversaw the construction, which terminated in October 1807. According to search and rescue historian Clayton Evans, writing in *Rescue at Sea*, "No evidence suggests that this boat was altered in any way for lifesaving, merely that it was chosen because of its inherent sea-keeping abilities and its popularity with local boatmen. Records do indicate, however, that one of Henry Greathead's lifeboats was purchased by the U.S. government in 1805. Although it is not known whether this particular boat was provided to the MHS or not." In the end, though, the new boat's description matched that of Greathead's *Original* uncannily.

She is rowed by ten men, double backed [ed. – probably should read "double banked"], but is fitted for twelve; and steered by two men with oars, one at each end, both ends being alike. Long poles are provided for the men to keep the boat from being drove broad side to the shore either in going off or landing. The poles, about six inches from their lower ends, increase in diameter so as to form a flat surface against the sand, otherwise they would sink into it, and be of no use. Seven hundred weight of the best cork would be sufficient for a boat of her dimensions, but that which was used inside her being indifferent, the weight of her cork is considerably increased. She draws very little water, and, when full, is able to carry twenty people. The boat is also to contend against the most tremendous sea and broken water, and boats of her construction have proved, in England, extremely useful in preserving the lives of shipwrecked mariners.

By 1810, the lifeboat had not yet been put to use, but then, as we shall see, several factors stood against that event taking place at that moment in American history. But, that fact aside, simply the construction and placement of the lifeboat along the Cohasset shore spoke volumes for the reputation of the Humane Society. As Mark Anthony DeWolfe Howe wrote in *The Humane Society of the Commonwealth of Massachusetts* in 1918, the "life-boat, built in 1807, was the first craft of its kind in America; and for more than forty years, until the United States Government took the first steps that led to the establishment of the Life-Saving Service, the Society stood alone in the work of rescuing seafarers wrecked on the coast of Massachusetts."

Finally, with local men poised to respond to shipwrecks and reach mariners in distress before they had to make the decision to swim to shore or take their chances on a crumbling vessel, the Humane Society had begun the evolution into a proactive lifesaving organization.

Chapter 5:
Opportunity Lost

In 1810, the Humane Society's annual report included six pages dedicated to the lifeboat then sitting on the Cohasset shore. In three years, though, the lifeboat had not been used a single time for rescue.

The lifeboat's placement in Cohasset in 1807 coincided with the commencement of one of the most stultifying, frustrating periods in history for American mariners. On June 10, 1807, the British warship HMS *Leopard* fired into the American warship USS *Chesapeake* off Norfolk, Virginia. The British believed that the American ship held deserters from their own Royal Navy. When the smoke cleared, that assumption proved to be true, as one wayward British sailor came forward. But the price for returning one sailor to a country with whom the United States had been at war within living memory was far too high for the American public, as three Chesapeake sailors died in the attack, and eighteen others received wounds.

The high seas had been a dangerous place for American ships for a decade. The Barbary Wars made the African coast a hazardous place to be, and unstable relations with France, peaking with the Quasi War in 1798, gave sailors another thought to keep in mind as they moved from port to port. In recent years, the United States had attempted to steer clear of both the French and British on the seas, as the foreign powers, historical enemies, had been doing everything in their power to disrupt each other's trade. British impressment of American sailors had been a longstanding problem as well. French disruption of American seagoing commerce leading up to the Quasi War had been so distressing that the new frigate *Constitution* was built at Hart's shipyard in Boston in 1797 to provide some measure of protection for the country's interests.

Despite all these issues, between 1804 and 1807, Boston benefited greatly as a neutral port through which the goods of both Great Britain and France flowed. When those nations were at war, American trading flourished. As long as the hostilities were not brought within sight or hearing distance of the United States, the crest of the wave would continue to glide along.

The *Chesapeake-Leopard* affair, though, took place too close to the coast of the United States for the American citizenry. They called to their leaders for action. In the end, though, the worst enemy of the American sailor would be his own federal government.

Immediately following the attack, President Thomas Jefferson ordered all British ships out of American ports. In December, Congress passed the Embargo Act of 1807. The act forbade American ships from entering foreign ports without the permission of the American president, strangely restraining citizens of the United States rather than seeking ways to punish or exclude ships flying under the flags of foreign powers. Moreover, the act required that American merchants post bonds worth twice the value of their ships and cargoes as guarantees the ships would not sail for foreign cities.

"The effect of the Embargo on the commerce of Boston is typical of its effect elsewhere," wrote John D. Forbes in "European Wars and Boston Trade, 1783-1815" in *The New England Quarterly*. "Legitimate commerce came very nearly to a dead stop. Customs receipts fell off by more than half as the ships came in from the seven seas to be tied up at their docks in Boston harbor."

"I have seen during the melancholy period of the non intercourse and the more distressing one of the late war," wrote Shubael Bell in "An Account of the Town of Boston Written in 1817" in *Bostonian Society Publications*, Second Series, "large ships and vessels at these wharves in such numbers that their sun burnt masts stripped of their cheering appendages, exhibited the appearance of a forest,

Several unpopular embargoes enacted during the presidency of Thomas Jefferson guaranteed that the Humane Society's first lifeboat would never live up to the hype the preceded its placement in Cohasset in 1807.

whose stately cedars had been deprived of their foliage by a destructive conflagration, or scath'd by the lightning of Heaven."

The enactment of the Embargo Act led to a major change in thinking in the United States. Unable to sail overseas, existing ships rotted at dockside. Sailing captains, especially those who specialized in high seas crossings, found work hard to come by. Coastwise shipping continued, but it did not have near the economic attraction as its transatlantic cousin. Shipbuilders, until that time thriving, stopped receiving any new orders. The repercussions resonated throughout that industry, to anchor forgers, sailmakers, suppliers of raw materials, and more.

Fewer ships in motion meant fewer shipwrecks. The Humane Society lifeboat at Cohasset continued to sit and wait.

Sadly, for American merchants and sailors, there was more to come. The federal government compounded the smothering legislation with two more acts aimed at stopping the flow of American goods into foreign ports. Just a month after the first Embargo Act, Congress passed its second. In January 1808, owners of whaling and coasting ships, those vessels tasked with moving goods along the East Coast from one American port to another, read with distress that they would now be required to post a bond similar to the one forced upon owners of transatlantic ships. They now had to put up money that doubled the value of their ships and cargo as insurance against the notion that they would use their vessels in foreign trade.

By March, New England had fallen into a deep economic depression. That month, President Jefferson signed into law the third and final Embargo Act, prohibiting the trading of any goods with any foreign interests. Further, the act gave port authorities the right to seize ships and cargoes from captains they suspected had even contemplated bringing their goods overseas. To remain economically viable, some American merchants returned reluctantly to the days of the American Revolution, when smuggling goods through enemy blockades was considered an act of patriotism. Now, although it was considered nearly treasonous, it became a way of life. The Embargo Acts were repealed in 1809, replaced by the Non-Intercourse Act, prohibiting trade with France and Great Britain. American capital moved from the shore to mills and factories, and eventually to opening up the vast natural resources of the unexplored west via a new transportation medium: the railroad.

The continued ill will between the United States and Great Britain, fueled partially by the trade wars, and deftly manipulated by Napoleon to France's advantage, led to a shooting war. President

James Madison and the United States declared war on Great Britain on June 1, 1812. "The effect of the War of 1812 upon American commerce was swift and grim," wrote Forbes. "Trade at Boston was paralyzed from the time when the British privateer Liverpool Packet was seen hovering off Cape Cod, soon after the opening of hostilities. Only armed privateers and ships of war ventured past the British blockading squadron." Once stifled by their own government, American merchants now watched as the once-again enemy British blockaded American ports. In some instances, the British even attacked ships in harbors, further depressing the industry. The War of 1812 raged well beyond that calendar year.

Affected by all these same forces, the Humane Society shifted its focus and its financial resources as well. While they concentrated on building and endowing hospitals, their lone lifeboat at Cohasset continued to sit unused. By 1813, the lifeboat, once a symbol of hope for the cause of humanity, was gone.

Chapter 6:
Interregnum

Lifeboat fever certainly gripped the attention of Bostonians in the years leading up to the construction of the first vessel. The Humane Society, though, while itself energized as a body with the lifeboat's potential lifesaving capabilities, had concomitantly been traveling down other roads.

A scant two years after its formation, the Society took steps to aid mariners shipwrecked on a far-off locale, Canada's Sable Island, off Cape Breton. The island, a thin, thirty-mile long sandbar barely supportive of life, human or wild, began claiming wrecks in 1583. The island's isolation and distance from potential rescuers left victims with ample space and time to ponder their last thoughts as starvation or hypothermia closed in. At the very least, a hut of refuge offered hope; at the most, the settlement of the island brought the likelihood of caring hands and warm hearths. Saving ships from disaster off Sable Island would boost mercantile returns, or at least keep them from diminishing.

As fate would have it, one the early supporters of the Humane Society and its efforts, Governor John Hancock, owned a considerable portion of Sable Island. (The island's historians surmise, in fact, that the wild horses that roam its beaches and grasslands today descend from stock left by Hancock's father Thomas in the 1750s). The Society approached the Governor with a proposal, asking that he ask the state legislature for funds to effect positive changes on the island in favor of

Rev. Dr. Jeremy Belknap helped change the focus of the Humane Society in its formative years, suggesting that the organization might turn its attention to the "sick-poor" of the city.

distressed sailors. The Governor made the pitch, to no avail. The Canadian government erected a lifesaving station on Sable Island in 1801.

In 1792, while the Sable Island issue was still on the table for the Trustees, another, joint effort was already in the works. A fraternal organization, the Boston Marine Society, formed in 1742 as a "fellowship club" of sea captains and ex-sea captains, asked the Humane Society to join them in petitioning Governor Hancock to consider the construction of a lighthouse at Truro "upon the High Land adjacent to Cape Cod Harbour." The trustees voted to support the cause, noting that a lighthouse would "preserve the lives and property of those who navigate the Bay of Massachusetts." A void of action on the part of the state led to a petition to the federal government at Philadelphia in 1796. With the help of the collector of customs for the port of Boston, General Benjamin Lincoln of Hingham, the lighthouse advanced from idea to physical reality, lighted for the first time in 1798.

The Society once again looked inward, at the health of the average citizen in Boston, thanks to prodding from historian and author Rev. Dr. Jeremy Belknap, "suggesting that some provision be made for the sick-poor, and particularly for exposed children," according to *The History of the Humane Society of Massachusetts*, 1845. Resulting votes supported consultation with "the Medical faculty, in order to most effectually provide for the sick-poor, for the assistance of lying-in women, and for foundlings." The same committee detailed to research that topic also recommended the collection of subscriptions for a public dispensary. On September 11, 1796, the Boston Dispensary opened under three operating principles: "The sick, without being pained on a separation from their families, may be attended and relieved in their own houses; The sick, can, in this way, be assisted at a less expense to the public than in any hospital, and; Those who have seen better days may be comforted without being humiliated; and all the poor receive the benefits of a charity, the more refined as it is the more secret."

Hospital building became a recurring theme for the Society. In 1801, an anonymous donor pledged four hundred dollars for the erection of "a building for those persons who are so unfortunate as to become insane." It took fifteen years, but finally, nudged by the Trustees of the Massachusetts General Hospital, the Society voted $5000 in support of "the Hospital for Lunatics, proposed to be established in this town, or its vicinity." In 1830, the Society revisited the notion of a lying-in hospital for single mothers. Working again with the Massachusetts General Hospital board and that of the Massachusetts Charitable Society, the Society saw that dream come to fruition, as the Boston Lying-In Hospital opened in 1834.

On June 12, 1798, the trustees discussed and voted on a proposal to determine ways to increase the safety of swimmers in the Cambridge River. The action came as a result of several recent deaths, including those of Harvard College students. The vote stated that the Trustees would send a committee to engage in conversation with a similar group from the college and the rest of the Cambridge community "respecting the expediency and practicability of erecting a bath upon the Cambridge river, for the purpose of preventing accidents that often occur in bathing in the open river." The Humane

Society granted $150 towards its construction, and by 1801, the new bath was in place.

Several of the old traditions started with the early days of the Society continued as the years pressed on. Between 1787 and 1817, the Society maintained its schedule of annual second Tuesday of June discourses on topics related to the medical and lifesaving goals of the organization.

And, of course, the Society's maritime safety goals remained paramount in their thoughts as they considered the dispersal of their raised funds. While the lifeboat placed in Cohasset in 1807 theoretically, if not yet practically, provided a tool for proactive rescue attempts, the Society was not in a position to rely on it as their sole weapon in the war against the sea. Hut of refuge construction continued. In 1792, the Society placed one at Stout's Creek in Truro, and in 1794, another at Great Point at Coskata on Nantucket, and another on the southern shore of that same island, most likely between Hummock and Long Ponds. Five years later, vessels traveling in and out of Quincy Harbor gained some measure of relief when the Society built a hut on Peddock's Island.

In 1802, a wave of construction and repair took place on Cape Cod: "One between Race Point and the head of Stout's creek, a mile from Peaked Hill, Cape Cod; One built by the Society in 1792, at Stout's Creek, having washed away for want of a proper foundation, another has been erected there; One on Nauset beach; One between Nauset and Chatham habours [sic]; One on the beach of Cape Malebarre [now Monomoy] on the sandy point of Chatham."

The first Stout's Creek hut had been built in a place with no anchoring beach grasses, according to a contemporary account, and as such, the winds had no trouble removing the sand from its base, and toppling it in January 1802. The timing could not have been worse. Six weeks later, three East India Company ships, the *Volusia*, *Ulysses* and *Brutus* foundered nearby. The crew of the *Brutus* reached shore safely, and within walking distance of the hut's remains, but, unable to find cover, they froze to death *en masse*.

Construction continued with two huts on "Duxburough" Beach in 1806 and continued throughout the century. Remote islands and desolate beaches remained priorities, despite ongoing vandalism.

In the years from 1787 to 1807, the Society effectively centralized news of heroism and bravery in eastern Massachusetts. The list of premiums awarded to every day citizens flowed in, leaving one to wonder how many similar instances of near tragedy had occurred in the years prior to the Society's founding.

> 1793. To S. Delano, Jr., for saving the crew of the ship Rodney, wrecked on Duxbury Beach, a Medal of Gold, valued at [British pounds] 4, 12, 4.
>
> 1794. To John Howell, George Dunton and John Brown, for saving the life of a son of Mr. Parker, who had fallen through the ice in the Mill Creek, $17.
>
> 1798. To Mr. Samuel Cox, on representation of Shubael Bell, Esq. for perilous efforts in saving John Thompson, upset in a boat, $10; And to the Man, who lives on Governor's Island, for receiving and relieving the same, $4.
>
> 1803. To Nehemiah Jaquith, aged 76, for saving the life of John Danley, of Tyngsborough, who had fallen through the ice in Merrimack River, $10.
>
> 1805. To William Power, commander of the schooner, Eleanor; to Archibald St. Dennis, commander of the schooner, Plough-Boy; and to John Power, commander of the Minerva, for their signal exertions in rescuing and receiving on board their respective vessels the passengers of the ship Jupiter, foundered at sea, - a Silver Can, each with suitable inscriptions, emblematical of the event, the value not to exceed the sum of thirty dollars each, together with the thanks of the Trustees to the crews of their respective vessels, $90.

As praiseworthy as the listings sounded, their prose was no match for the numerous letters attesting to moments of selflessness that reached the attention of the Trustees each year. Sometimes, as they learned, though, sorrow won out over courageousness and good intentions.

Cohasset, 24th March, 1808
Reverend Sir,

Your son observed to me, it was your wish to see some statement of the melancholy event that occurred at Cohasset, on the 3d inst. To the family of the two captain Snows, (brothers) in said town...

On the day of the above date, two sons, from seven to ten years of age, playing on the ice, (which was sufficient to support them near the shore, but becoming weaker toward the channel,) fell through at a good distance, but in sight of the house, and their mothers, who instantly flew to their assistance; passing on about fifty feet from the bank, one of the mothers broke in; her little daughter, of eleven years, followed and fell through, near the mother; the other Mrs. Snow, finding it impossible to render them any assistance, very judiciously ran for the nearest neighbours, for assistance, and the nearest help, which was myself, and others, standing on a wharf, nearly half a mile from them. We immediately ran to their assistance, and to my surprise, discovered three heads above water; in approaching them, a creek intervened, catching a pine rail in my hand, I crossed the mouth, whilst my companions ran around the head of it, the ice being tender; but observing one of the children sinking, was induced to take the risk, and was fortunate enough to get within ten feet of it, before the ice gave way, till the persons came off with a boat on the ice, and took in Mrs. Snow, and the others that were nearest to the bank. Extending a pole to me, I grasped it with one hand, and held the child by the other, till they dragged us to the boat, and took us in; presuming ourselves safe, judge my surprise, when in, to discover the boat leaking to such degree, that it went down from under us in less than thirty seconds. Entangled with the ice, about sixty feet from the bank of the meadow, which we could neither approach for the ice, nor being strong enough for those to come to our assistance, without getting into the same distress, which some of them did. After long struggling, they all succeeded to get on the ice, except myself, Mrs. Snow, and one other man, and the children, who all drowned. Finding such entanglement at the edge of the ice, I swam for the sunken boat again, where we all remained, till they went some distance to the house, and uncorded beds and brought lines, which being thrown off the edge of the ice, I caught the end, and perceiving the woman's hair above water, seized it; they pulled us to the edge of the ice, at the same time pushing toward us a long ladder. I passed one arm through the lower slat, and clinching the woman in my arms, they dragged us through the ice, till it became strong enough for a person to come out, and haul us on to the ladder, Mrs. Snow perfectly senseless. Being carried to the house and stripped, thrown into warm blankets, the process of friction was commenced, and at the same time constant application of hot cloths, with vessels filled with hot water, which succeeded in restoring the circulation, in a short time. The children were recovered in half an hour after they sunk, and some effort made on one of them to resuscitate, but without effect – the water being near the freezing point, and the atmosphere about the same, these bodies were too much chilled to promise success, by perseverance.

The scene was distressing and melancholy; for some time I expected eight or ten persons would perish in the presence of twenty smart active men, well acquainted with the element we were struggling with, and not more than sixty feet distant, for the want of means; for as fast as they approached us, they were in the same difficulty.

Considering the cold, it is astonishing that the woman and children remained alive till our arrival, which must have been about half an hour, and after the boat sunk nearly a quarter more, and myself was so chilled, that I could not reach the house without assistance. The water was part salt and part fresh, about ten feet deep.

Mrs. Snow's life is not at present in danger; but being dragged about the boat and ice, with her own struggles, she will require time to recover perfect health, if she ever does.

S. Stephenson

Stephenson received $10 from the Humane Society for his efforts. In other instances, as reported here by the man who would later become Boston's famous "Ice King," the results of such breathtaking exertions were as satisfying as they were relieving.

Boston, January 10th, 1814
Sir,

I have understood the Humane Society are desirous of ascertaining the facts relative to the rescue of two children from drowning by Mr. William Savage. As I was an eye witness to the transaction, I am able to give the particulars, and I do it with the more pleasure, because they are so highly honourable to the good feelings of Mr. Savage.

About two months since, I was sitting with Mr. S. in his counting-room on the North Battery Wharf, when we heard a cry of *"some body overboard."* Savage immediately rushed out of the counting-room, followed by me. In his way down to the wharf *as he run* he took off his coat, he could not relieve himself of any thing else. When I came to the wharf, I saw two children in the water; Mr. S. had jumped over before I reached the spot. He first took the largest, about four or five years old, and swam to the wharf, where it was received by some of the by-standers. The other was in great danger, having its head entirely under water, owing to the buoyancy of the cloathes, and must have suffocated in a few moments, but the immediate exertions of Mr. Savage saved that also. The last was somewhat bruised and bloody about the head.

The children were about twenty feet from the wharf, carried off, either by the tide of their own struggles. I should think the water must have been about seven feet deep, and I think the youngest at least, if not both, would have perished, but for the prompt exertions of Mr. Savage.

I have the honour to be, your humble servant,

Frederic Tudor

Savage, Tudor's cousin, received $10 from the Humane Society. He was not the first lifesaving hero recognized by the Humane Society, and he would not be the last. The Golden Age of the Humane Society lifesaver was still ahead, but it would take the determination and drive of a special man to usher it in.

Chapter 7:
The Right Man for the Job

On December 12, 1775, eight months after the "shot heard 'round the world" was fired at Lexington heralding the commencement of the military operations of the American Revolution, Benjamin Rich was born in Truro, near the end of Cape Cod. He would rise to be one of his community's greatest sons, perhaps spurred by the tales of the townsfolk of his youth. "When the Revolution put an end to their maritime enterprise," wrote Agnes Edwards in *Cape Cod New and Old*, "the Truro fishermen, like the rest of the Cape Codders, melted up their mackerel leads for bullets, and made a record so valiant that it will never be forgotten as long as American history is read." Twenty-eight men, representing the twenty-three houses that comprised the town, gave their lives in the Revolution.

Following the maritime traditions of his forbearers and contemporaries, Rich headed to sea as a cabin boy at thirteen years of age. He took part in the burgeoning Canton trade, as the young United States capitalized on the recent controlled opening of the Chinese port. He made four major voyages over the next six years in that position, and in 1794, at age 19, he made his first passage to the Far East as a ship's master, a calling he would follow for the next six years.

Like all overseas merchants of the time, the young man faced a variety of dangers while heading from port to port. In 1798 the fledgling United States entered into the Quasi-War with France without a national navy, leaving its merchant seamen virtually unprotected. Pirates still roamed the high seas in search of plunder, especially the supposedly easily-attainable goods to be pulled from vessels returning from the Far East with furniture, rugs, clothing and spices.

Rich's most intense encounter took place off Algiers. There, "he was attacked...by two French privateers both of which, with his characteristic intrepidity, he fought a whole summer's day; and at last, when his shot was all expended and he had charged his cannon with whatever he could find on board, he succeeded in beating them off," wrote Reverend Alexander D. D. Young in a discourse on Rich's life in 1851.

On March 31, 1800, at age 24, Benjamin Rich married Susanna Heath of Roxbury, the act that forced a change in lifestyle that pulled him away from the helm of his ships. In 1801, he retired from the sea and began a new phase of his life, as one of the leading commerce experts in Boston. He had prepared himself, said Young, "by personal observations of various parts of the world and large intercourse with the inhabitants of other climes and intimate acquaintance with the products of foreign lands."

In 1811, Rich embarked on a career in philanthropy, that year being chosen as a Trustee of the Humane Society. His association with the Society would last for 33 years.

Perhaps Rich's heartfelt dedication to the Society's causes stemmed from the loss of his younger brother Nehemiah at sea in 1804. Maybe his thoughts returned to the gallant men of his hometown, who spent their lives on the decks of ships at sea to help keep their families fed, and took up arms when called upon to defend them. Or perhaps a deeper, inherent sense of bravery and nobility of spirit drew him to that organization. In May of 1818 Rich displayed his own personal courage following an explosion aboard a Canton packet tied up in Boston Harbor. Focusing solely on the fact that lives were in danger, the 42-year old leapt onto the deck through the dancing flames, disregarding the possibility of secondary explosions, and rescued the crew. Or, maybe, he simply understood all too well the risks of life at sea from his own experiences as a sailor, and valued the measure of protection the Humane Society charitably offered to his brethren off the Massachusetts coast.

During the first decade of the nineteenth century, the Riches started their family. In 1802, Susanna gave birth to their first child, Benjamin, Jr., who grew up to join his father in the family business, Benjamin Rich and Son, but sadly died an early death by consumption in the West Indies in 1829. A second child, daughter Susanna, died the year following her birth, while a second son, Samuel Heath Rich, known by the epithet "Gentleman Sam, tall and fine," died in 1846 in Calcutta, by one account, or in Hong Kong, by another. Julia Rich Hogan, writing in *The Rich Family Association Kinfolk*, states that "two daughters, Susan and Elizabeth, survived the smallpox epidemic in Boston and later married," (p.12), while Shebnah Rich, in *Truro, Cape Cod, or Land Marks and Sea Marks*, tells the story of two gravesites "upon the steep hill top, northwest of Ebenezer Freeman's house, in a little enclosure" where "are buried two members of [Benjamin Rich's] family who died in Boston of small-pox." One other daughter definitely survived to marry the successful Charles Larkin of the firm of Larkin and Stackpole. But it was Benjamin and Susannah's son Charles that provided perhaps the most dramatic moment in the life of the young family. Rich received the following letter from Roxbury on May 2, 1821:

> Dear Sir:
>
> You request me to give you a circumstantial account of the accident which happened to your son Charles, on April 6th.
>
> Charles and two of his fellow schoolfellows, William H. Fowle, between 12 and 13 years old, and Henry R. Dearborn, between 11 and 12 years old, were playing by a small pond near the schoolhouse; Charles fell from a projecting rock into the deepest part of the pond, where the water was then about seven feet deep, it being increased by the melted snow. Charles sunk and rose so that the top and back part of his head were above the surface of the water. The two lads who were near tried to reach him with

their hands, and to throw the ends of their handkerchiefs to him, but they could not reach him. They then threw a small dry tree into the water very near him, but he took no notice of it, neither could they make him hear. The elder boy then ran for something else, he brought the branch of a tree, which the younger lad catching hold of, jumped with it in his hands, into the water where it was not so deep as his height, reached it to Charles, who was wholly under water except his hands, which were raised above his head. He put the end of the branch into Charles' hand, but he appeared not to be sensible of it till it was rubbed forward and backward against his hand; he then seized it very fast and the lad drew Charles towards him and carried him out of the pond. Charles' strength was much exhausted, his countenance changed, and for a short time he was not conscious of his situation. The lads brought him home in their arms. The means that were afterwards used, I believe, have been mentioned to you. I greatly regret the accident, but feel thankful to heaven that he is spared to you; and that he may long be spared, and afford you all that satisfaction and comfort, that a good and promising child is calculated to give his parents, is the ardent hope of

Yours, with much esteem,

Jacob N. Knapp.

Later that year, Rich had the honor of presenting William Fowle and Henry Dearborn, fellow students of master Charles at Knapp's Academy, with the Humane Society's gold lifesaving medal for saving the life of his own child. Charles grew to become a Congregational minister in Springfield, Illinois, described by Shebnah Rich as "a cultivated Christian gentleman, social and genial."

In 1829, while serving in his nineteenth year as a trustee, Benjamin Rich had the distinction of being elected as the Ninth President of the Massachusetts Humane Society, a position he would hold until 1843. During his tenure he spearheaded the launching of the Society into what historian Mark Anthony DeWolfe Howe described as the "golden age" of the Society, described as lasting from 1840 until the successful restructuring of the federal United States Life-Saving Service by Sumner Increase Kimball in 1871.

The Society had built the first American lifeboat in Nantucket in 1807, placing it in Cohasset that year. The boat remained there until 1813, but succeeding that date no records of lifeboats along the Massachusetts coast exist until 1840. Although the Society had successfully maintained a series of houses of refuge along the coast since 1787, in January of 1840, Rich and the board of trustees expressed their desire to re-enter the world of organized shore-based lifesaving of mariners in distress at sea.

The timing was by no means arbitrary. December 1839 had been one of the worst months on record for the New England seaman. Three successive storms over fourteen days decimated the coast, leaving hundreds of Massachusetts residents dead, orphaned or widowed. First, on December 14, a pleasantly calm day beckoned mariners to sea. After midnight, though, northeast winds began to blow and snow started to fall. When the winds shifted to the southeast and gained in power, many of the ships still off the coast were blown back towards it. By noon on the 15th, a full gale was underway. Historian Sidney Perley described the scene as such in *Historic Storms of New England*:

> All along the coast the harbor scenes consisted of the vessels tossing on the darkened stormy waters and blown by the wind and thrown about by the waves, being watched with intense interest and anxiety by the dwellers along the coast, who saw the fate of the hapless mariners in the awful breakers on the lee shore. Many people with willing hands and noble, stout hearts hastened to afford assistance if chance should offer, or it could avail. One after another the

vessels were seen to drift, and apparently hurry on to destruction, while many silent, earnest prayers ascended from the throngs on the beaches in behalf of the impotent mariners. Some of the crafts turned over and went down at their anchors bottom up, with the crews, who were seen no more. The fearful end of many vessels, however, was checked by cutting away the masts. Others were steered for sandy beaches, upon which the wind drove them, and with assistance from the people on shore, the lives of most of the sailors were saved. Several of them were dashed upon rocks and shivered to atoms in a moment, in some instances the crews being saved in various ways by the strong arms of mariners who had battled with the waves and storms for years. As night came on the storm seemed rather to increase than diminish, and the wind blew more violently than it had before or during the storm, darkness with all its gloom settling down over the scene that was never to be effaced from the memory of those that witnessed it.

The storm continued into Monday, with its greatest destruction coming on Sunday night. "The whole shore of Massachusetts was strewn with wrecks and dead bodies, and the harbors of Newburyport, Salem, Marblehead, Boston, Cohasset, Plymouth and Cape Cod were almost literally filled with disabled vessels," wrote Perley.

The anonymous author of the pamphlet "Awful Calamities: or, the Shipwrecks of December, 1839" declared Gloucester to be the scene of the most heartrending disasters.

More than FIFTY vessels were either driven ashore, dismasted, or carried to sea, and the loss of lives could not have fallen much short of FIFTY. From one end of the beach to the other, nothing could be seen but pieces of broken wrecks; planks and spars, shattered into a thousand splinters; ropes and sails, parted and rent; flour, fish, lumber and a hundred other kinds of lading and furniture, soaked and broken; with here and there a mangled and naked body of some poor mariner; and in one instance that of a woman lashed to the windlass bitts of a Castine schooner, lay all along the beach, while off, thirty yards, with the surf breaking over them every moment and freezing in the air, lay nearly a score of lost vessels; all together forming a picture which it is in vain to attempt to copy in words.

The chronicler, though, found words to describe the deeds of other men who no doubt caught the attention of the Trustees of the Humane Society. "In the midst of this scene of terror, the hardy and noble fishermen of Cape Ann, fully proved that a sailor's jacket seldom covers a craven heart. They manned two boats, the Custom House boat and the Van Buren; and fearlessly risked their lives for the safety of their fellow creatures. Vessel after vessel was visited by them; they made their way over the tops of mountain-waves, and through the gaping chasms of the hungry waters; and from the very teeth of greedy death, plucked many a poor, despairing, and exhausted fellow; bringing him safe to shore."

The act of heroism was not the only one recorded during the storm. The Humane Society recognized "Joseph Howard, Samuel Parker and seven others for boarding the wreck of the brig Independence, during the gale of 15th Dec. last, and taking thence the crew from the rigging at much hazard, five dollars each," a total of $45. Then, to "Isaac Small, who, during the same severe gale, went on board the brig Austin, wrecked at Provincetown, and at the peril of his own life, and signal exertions, rescued a disabled seaman, the President was authorized to present a Quadrant, with a suitable inscription, in token of approbation of his heroic conduct."

The list continued. "To Gorham Riggs, Donald Ryder, and nine other persons, who, during the same dreadful tempest of Dec. 15th, went on board a vessel in Gloucester Harbor, and were the means, under Divine Providence, of saving several persons, five dollars each." Finally, "To Samuel Pierce, and his Son, for assistance rendered to the crew of the schooner Scio, when driven on shore at Wellfleet, in the gale of 15th Dec., five dollars."

The following Saturday, snow began to fall in Baltimore, Maryland. It reached Boston the following day, and on Monday morning, the 23rd, howling northeast winds joined the elements in stopping cold the railroads and driving ashore ships that had survived the previous storm. The storm, read "Awful Calamities," was "less severe than that of the 15th, although sufficiently violent to have obtained under other circumstances, the name of a terrible hurricane." On Boston's North Shore that Monday, Plum Island could not contain the storm's surge, eroding away in wide swaths. Sand hills vanished from some places, and grew anew to the same heights in others. And it was there that the brig *Pocahontas* came ashore.

The *Pocahontas*, of Newburyport, had sailed from Cadiz, Spain, in October under Captain James Cook. Captain Nathaniel Brown, the proprietor of a popular hotel on the island, espied the dismasted vessel about a half mile from his establishment on an offshore sandbar, and hurried to the scene. Three men could be seen clinging to the wreck; by the time citizens from Newburyport could trudge through the marsh separating the island from the mainland (the turnpike had been severely damaged by the storm), only one sailor remained. Several courageous men rushed to the shore with Captain Brown's skiff, endeavoring to row to the ship to save who was most likely a fellow townsman. The snow obscured the man's identity, and the towering waves frustrated their attempt. The sea washed the man off the bowsprit, he regained his hold, and then was lost to the waves again. Moments later the wreck broke loose and drifted ashore. A man formerly unseen yet lashed to the wreckage took a few breaths ashore, but became the thirteenth and final victim of the shipwreck. Not a single man survived to tell the tale. Captain Cook had sailed the breadth of the Atlantic only, noted Perley, "to perish within sight of the smoke ascending from his own hearthfire."

At noon on that same day, the bark *Lloyd* of Portland, Maine, sailing from Havana to Boston, ran aground on Nantasket Beach. With the fore and mainmasts gone and the mizzenmast snapped in two, the ship's fate had already been determined. Six men boarded the ship's longboat and attempted to row to shore, but were drowned when their boat was upset by the sea. Another man, an Englishman named George Scott, floated ashore on an oar into the waiting arms of the chagrined people of Hull. Three more sailors lashed themselves to the vessel, hoping the bark would hold together until the gale petered out. For two of those men, the end came quickly, as their restraints proved no match for the power of the sea.

Captain Daniel Mountfort, though, held on as long as humanly possible. Torn from the rigging and dashed onto the deck, his bruised and battered body refused to surrender. Sailors from another wrecked ship, the *Charlotte*, awaited their chance, and then dashed in their ship's boat to the *Lloyd*. On their third attempt they grabbed the insensible ship's master and transported him to shore. Well removed from the village, the people of Hull hastened Mountfort to the nearest Humane Society hut of refuge and initiated the same lifesaving efforts they and their kin had been practicing for decades. Their efforts were in vain. Portland, Maine, lost its oldest and most respected sea captain when the last breath left the lungs of Captain Mountfort. Eight others died with him, Scott being the only survivor.

Four days later, around 11 p.m. on Friday the 27th, the winds began again, this time from the east-southeast. As New England residents worriedly listened to the howling gale, they wondered if the rapture had indeed arrived. In Boston the ship *Columbiana* parted her lines and drove through the Charlestown Bridge under the power of the wind. The storm's surge flooded the low-lying sections of the city, carrying away cargoes on wharves awaiting transport. The brig *Adelaide*, which had just undergone repairs for damage wrought in the first storm, lost part of its bow. At Salem, the schooner *Pocasset* smashed its bowsprit through a cooper's shop. In Newburyport, where tides rose to their highest point in three decades, ships sank at anchor. At Provincetown, salt mills blew down and residents were forced to flee their homes during the storm's most intense period, between four and six in the morning.

The author of "Awful Calamities" summed up the aftermath:

> From the foregoing account, it appears that 1 barque, 17 brigs, 68 schooners, and 4 sloops were lost in the three gales; and the estimated number of lives

destroyed at the same time are from 150 to 200. It was supposed 50 were lost at Gloucester alone in the first storm. Besides this, 23 ships and barques, 22 brigs, 168 schooners, and 5 sloops, were dismasted, driven ashore, or greatly injured in some other way. The destruction of property must have been near $1,000,000. We do not suppose we have ascertained the loss of near all the vessels which have been destroyed by these tornadoes. Many were foundered at sea; and some went ashore and to pieces, so that no intelligible record of their loss is left behind.

The storms cast a pall across coastal New England unmatched in the region's settled history. "Into the short period of fourteen days, the agony of years was pressed," quoted "Awful Calamities." "Many who entered the month of December with a fair prospect of enjoying a "happy new year," and perhaps a long life, now sleep in the bosom of the great deep with the sea-weed wrapped around them, or have been tossed on shore by the bellowing surges, and all bruised and mangled, have been followed, perhaps by strangers, to an untimely grave."

For the Trustees of the Humane Society, the lessons were obvious. Where men had been able, they launched boats from shore in attempts to rescue mariners in distress, under the direst of conditions. The people of Massachusetts were prepared to risk their own lives so that others might potentially live their lives longer. Disaster struck most distressingly where proper lifeboats were unavailable, as in the case of the *Pocahontas* off Plum Island. There, said Perley, "The men could only look at each other through the falling snow, from land to sea, from sea to land, and each realized how impotent they all were." In the one recorded instance where a Humane Society hut of refuge was utilized, it was inadequate. Had a lifeboat been available on the Hull shore, at least some of the crew of the *Lloyd* might have survived the storm.

The trustees met in January 1840 and appointed a committee to examine the lifeboat question. The inquiry was not intended to determine whether or not lifeboats were needed along the

Massachusetts shore; instead, it was to determine whether or not the Society could adequately provide them. Under the guidance of Captain Benjamin Rich, the Society would transform the state's lifesaving system back from reactive to proactive.

Chapter 8:
Into the Golden Age

The committee formed at the January 1840 meeting of the Trustees of the Humane Society quickly found their answer. The coffers of the Society would not yield sufficient funds to construct new boats. But the Humane Society was not the only body in the state that had watched the carnage of the storms of December 1839.

On March 21, 1840 the Massachusetts legislature voted, "That there be allowed and paid out of the Treasury of the Commonwealth, to the President and Trustees of the Massachusetts Humane Society, the sum of five thousand dollars, for the purpose of furnishing Life Boats, to be stationed at the most exposed parts of the seacoast within this Commonwealth, and that a warrant be drawn therefor. And that the said Society be requested to report to the Governor and Council their expenditure of the funds appropriated by this Resolve, together with the number and stations of the boats." The Trustees received the news at their meeting the following month. The resolve was signed by Robert Charles Winthrop, Speaker of the House of Representatives, and Daniel Putnam King, Senate President, and approved by Governor Marcus Morton. Morton had been defeated in the November 1840 gubernatorial election, and stood to be replaced by Governor-elect John Davis on January 7. The timing indicates, therefore, that the resolution had its roots prior to the final vote, again most likely in rapid response to the storms of December.

The state of Massachusetts, led by Governor Marcus Morton, supported the plea of Humane Society President Benjamin Rich to make the Massachusetts coast safer through the construction of several volunteer-manned lifeboats.

The Trustees, working under the direction of Captain Benjamin Rich and Henry Oxnard, Esquire, began the process of contracting for the construction of the lifeboats. A gap exists in the story of the Humane Society, due to the Great Boston Fire of 1872, which destroyed many of its records. Due to that gap, the details of those lifeboat construction contracts have been lost.

The work progressed quickly. By August, letters had been sent to the selectmen of the towns chosen to receive the lifeboats, signed by the Society's President, Captain Rich.

> Boston, August 10, 1840
> To Hon. George B. Upton, and the Selectmen of Nantucket:
>
> Gentlemen: With the money granted by the State, the Massachusetts Humane Society have a Life Boat finished, which they wish placed in the best

situation to relieve shipwrecked mariners on your island. They wish you to select ten active men, one of whom to be appointed as chairman, (sending in their names, which are to be recorded in the books of the Society,) to take charge of said boat, any five or six of whom being present can manage her. But their services must be considered as granted voluntarily for humane and charitable purposes. And whenever any meritorious act is performed by the volunteers in the boat, in rescuing lives, they shall be suitably rewarded on a full representation of the same to the Society

It is necessary that a suitable house should be built to protect the boat from the weather; the bill of which will be paid on presentment."

The Nantucket selectmen chose Tuckernuck Island, off Smith's Point on the remote western end of the island, for the construction of the first boathouse and placement of their first lifeboat. Daniel T. Dunham, an island resident, took responsibility for the boat.

On January 4, 1841, the Society, represented by Oxnard and Francis Parkman, wrote a letter to Governor John Davis detailing the successful completion of the work outlined in the Resolve of March 21, 1840. The funds delivered to the Society sufficiently covered the construction of eleven lifeboats. Ten of the boats paid for by the State fell directly under the watchful eyes of the Trustees: the Tuckernuck boat; one at Edgartown, on Martha's Vineyard; one each on three of Cape Cod's most dangerous stretches of sand, at Nauset Beach in Eastham, at Cahoon's Hollow in Wellfleet, and at Truro near Highland Lighthouse; one at Cohasset Harbor; another on the shipwreck hotspot of Nantasket Beach; one in Lynn; one at Gloucester; and one at "Sandy Bay," now Rockport. An eleventh boat, paid for through the treasury of the Society, was placed in Scituate.

The final lifeboat constructed using the appropriated funds from the state government was placed on Plum Island, but rather than being under the control of the Humane Society and its trustees, fell instead to the domain of the Newburyport Marine Society. That organization, patterned on the Boston and Salem marine societies, began operation in 1772, undertaking the mission of caring for its members, retired and aging sea captains from the town, and their families. Its focus expanded to include the centralization of local nautical knowledge, the construction of day marks at either end of the island in 1783, and, in 1787, the erection of two huts of refuge along the shore for stranded mariners, in direct response to the actions of the Humane Society elsewhere along the Massachusetts coast that year. By the 1840s, the Newburyport Marine Society was confidently in a position to receive and oversee the use of the last lifeboat.

"The whole number of boats thus provided is twelve," wrote Parkman and Oxnard, "all of which are furnished with oars, buckets and four bars of iron for ballast. These can be taken out when it is necessary to transport the boats to any distance. A house, twenty feet long, eight feet and a half wide, shingled on the top, and battened to the sides has been built for each boat."

Of the $5,000 received, the Society dedicated $4,962.72 to the lifeboats. The balance of $37.28 joined a grant of $200 from the Newburyport Marine Society to leave a positive balance in the reserves of the Society.

The following week, the State commended the work of the Society through a letter from Joseph Grinnell of the Governor's Council, and suggested that the Trustees consider publishing the list of lifeboats, with precise locations, in the region's newspapers, "so that shipwrecked vessels might direct their course, if in their power, to such places." The Society agreed on the course of action, while the Legislature returned to work.

On March 17, 1841, Governor Davis approved another $1350 for three more lifeboats. This time, though, the resolve specified locations: Race Point in Provincetown, Chatham and Nantucket. As with the first resolve, the government required confirmation of expenditures. Captain Rich responded on behalf of the Society the following January. Sadly, by this time, Henry Oxnard, who had worked so diligently on the lifeboat projects, had taken seriously ill, and had retreated to Europe in an attempt at convalescence. By 1843, he would be gone.

The Society had followed the State's instructions to the letter, providing boats for the three locations. But, according to Rich, they had taken the liberty of extending the value of the funds appropriated. "Finding another boat was absolutely necessary, and being strongly solicited from the town of Plymouth," he stated, "I prevailed on the mechanics to give in a part of their labor, and build the boats fifty dollars less each, which enabled me to provide a fourth boat for that station, by the Humane Society paying the balance, $175.86, as per account annexed."

Inevitably, the day arrived when the new lifesaving network would be tested. In early October 1841, a gale arose that not only did so, it also pulled directly on the heartstrings of the President of the Humane Society. From Nantucket to Portland, a mixed storm of rain, snow and wind smashed the coast and devastated the fishing fleets of the states of Massachusetts, New Hampshire and Maine. On Nantucket, a portion of Siasconset Beach eroded away nearby the lighthouse, two ropewalks, the observatory and several chimneys were blown down and water flooded the streets.

The ship *Maine*, tied up in Portsmouth, New Hampshire, parted her lines and began to drift. The sustained tempest prodded the vessel continually to the south until it struck heavily on the rocks off the Cohasset shore, coming to rest in pieces at Scituate. The captain, his daughter, one crewman and five passengers perished as a result.

At Cape Ann, volunteer lifesavers attempted to get their Humane Society lifeboat underway, but damage sustained to the bottom during launch necessitated a permanent return to shore. But the worst of the damage was done on Massachusetts' other famed cape. Between Chatham and Truro, more than forty vessels came ashore, yielding about fifty dead bodies. Dennis lost twenty-six young men, eighteen of whom had attended school together.

The Truro fishing fleet was on George's Bank when the storm struck, and *en masse* headed for the steadying rays of Highland Light. One by one, the ships were taken by the sea. In all, fifty-seven young men on seven ships lost their lives. Among them were 29-year-old Benjamin Rich on the *Cincinnatus*, Zoheth Rich, 25, on the *General Harrison*, and 18-year-old Jessie, 26-year-old Elisha, 24-year-old Joseph, and 22-year-old William Rich - the last three brothers - on the *Altair*. The storm took Captain Benjamin Rich's townsfolk, and it took his kinfolk. In the wake of the devastation, Rich tirelessly walked the streets of Boston, conscripting almost $6,000 for the relief of the twenty-seven widows and fifty-one children of the lost men. In all, the population of Cape Cod included more than 900 widows of the sea by 1841.

Just two months later, it was the mettle of the men of Hull that was challenged. On December 17, the ship *Mohawk* of Liverpool was caught in a gale off Nantasket Beach. In the consuming darkness, Captain Moses Binney Tower gathered his volunteer crew and headed for the vessel. In the confusion, he did not notice that a 15-year-old boy had leapt into the fray until the lifeboat was well underway. Unable to turn back, Tower led his crew to the rescue of a dozen men. The youngster, Joshua James, would become one of the most decorated lifesavers in Humane Society and American history.

While the rescue validated the joint plan of the State and the Society to guard the Massachusetts shore with lifesaving equipment, the October and December 1841 rescue attempts underscored the need for a different form of vigilance. "In the gale of the 17th of December last," wrote Rich in his January 1842 report, "when the ship Mohawk was cast on shore at Nantasket Beach, when the life boat stationed there was launched into the surf, and, in endeavoring to save the crew, she was driven on the rocks and badly stove. Since which she has been brought to the city and is now repairing, will be finished soon and re-placed in its proper station, the cost of which will be from sixty to eighty dollars. These boats will be constantly wanting repairs, painting &c. &c., and it will be necessary that a small appropriation should be made for that purpose..." Twenty-eight lives had been saved to date, at the expense of at least two thoroughly damaged boats. The return on the proposed investment to repair the boats was, of course, immeasurable. The Legislature resolved later that spring to pay the Humane Society "the sum of six hundred dollars, for the safe keeping, preserving and repairing of the several life-boats belonging to the Commonwealth."

With lifeboat stations now established from Cape Ann to the islands, and the notion of recurring maintenance costs impressed upon the state's legislators, Captain Benjamin Rich began his fade into the background. Now entering his late sixties, he felt that the time

72

had arrived to allow a younger man to take the role as the Society's leader, for he as well had other goals in life he hoped to achieve. A highly religious man, he had already raised the necessary funds to preserve his church's spire, when the need arose for a new fence around the building. Through his efforts, that fence soon stood.

Responding to Rich's letter of resignation on 1844, the Trustees of the Society expressed their appreciation for his devoted decades of service. "You have been instrumental in providing for the wants and relief of the needy and shipwrecked mariners. You have superintended the building and the localities of our life-boats. To yourself...belong(s) emphatically the praise of this grand scheme of relief to the brave mariner in the hour of dreadful peril. Enjoy the high estimate you hold in this community, as a merchant and a philanthropist. Accept our best wishes for your future happiness and usefulness; and when your sun sets, may it be in the serenity of a green old age."

The Rich family continued his tradition of involvement with coastal lifesaving. Captain Mulford Rich of Wellfleet, who took immediate control of the Cahoon's Hollow lifeboat in 1841, boarded twenty-five wrecks and saved twenty-nine lives over the course of his life, earning a Society gold medal for the rescue of the crew of the *Franklin* in 1849. Captain Benjamin Swett Rich served as superintendent of the United States Life-Saving Service's Fifth Life-Saving District, along the coasts of Delaware and Virginia, from 1875 until his death in 1900. Anthony Atwood Rich contracted and built the federal Cahoon's Hollow Life-Saving Station in Wellfleet in 1885.

On June 3, 1851, Captain Benjamin Rich, Ninth President of the Humane Society of the Commonwealth of Massachusetts, died at his Boston home at 75 years, 5 months, and 22 days old. The next morning all of the ships in Boston Harbor dropped their flags to half-mast in his honor.

Chapter 9:
A New Breed of Hero

The combined actions of the Massachusetts legislature and the Humane Society to line the state's coast with lifeboats provided the tools needed to save lives from shipwreck, but no such tools could be effective without craftsmen trained and willing to use them. The Society's plans called for "ten active men, one of whom to be appointed chairman" of each boat positioned on the coast. That local "chairman" would eventually become known as the "keeper" of the Society's boat or boats in a given community.

An "active man" in Massachusetts in the 1840s was usually an entrepreneur, someone who had gained a great measure of respect within his community for embodying the ideals that led Senator Henry Clay of Kentucky to define the "self-made man" in 1832. "Almost every manufactory known to me," said the War Hawk, "is in the hands of enterprising self-made men, who have whatever wealth they possess by patient and diligent labor." Such men, once they comfortably solidified their wealth, shared their abundant energy with their communities, driving improvements to infrastructure, taking important primary roles in town government and enabling other young men to strive for greatness by offering their own examples of leadership.

Moses Binney Tower, the first keeper of the Humane Society's boats in Hull, was one such man. He was born in Hingham on April 26, 1814, the second child of Moses and Mary Binney Tower. Moses the younger spent his childhood at the family home on Hobart Street on Great Hill, where his father kept a farm. When he was just eleven years old, he lost his mother, who died two days short of what would have been her thirty-fifth birthday. Six months later, on Christmas Day, 1825, his father remarried, exchanging vows with Abigail Andrews Gould of Hull.

Moses could not have been very happy at home. The family never had much money, but nevertheless had grown to number six children by 1828. Moses, by then fourteen, did not want to spend the rest of his life tied to the soil, so he left home to commune with his first real love, the sea. It was a relationship that would last for the next seventy years.

He joined the crew of a mackerel fishing schooner in Hingham Harbor, starting out as a cook. As the years went by, he learned all he could about the business, becoming captain and finally owner of his own ship. His penniless childhood had served him well; he understood the value of money at an early age and the virtues of saving it as well.

He also excelled at making money. On June 10, 1838, Moses married Olive Gould Cushing of Hull. The next year he spent $800 on the purchase of the venerable Robert Gould house on the corner of Mt. Pleasant and Main streets, a large two-story dwelling that had been standing since 1675. He began to expand the house immediately and converted it into one of the seaside community's first hotels, and the only one in the heart of Hull Village, the Nantascot House. The innkeeper specialized in letting boats to amateur fishermen.

According to James Lloyd Homer, who wrote a series of letters to newspaper readers in Boston from Hull during the mid-1840s, Tower was "visited every summer by thousands of persons - men, women and children - from Boston, Hingham, Weymouth, Quincy, Dorchester, Dedham, Roxbury, and other towns, who spend a day with him at his well-regulated establishment, and then depart with feelings satisfied, and health improved. His charges are reasonable and his exertions to please untiring. He is a 'prosperous gentleman,' and keeps an excellent free-and-easy temperance house."

But Tower did much more in Hull than simply run a hotel. He became a one-man beautification committee, planting American Elm trees in the town cemetery and outside of his hotel. He served Hull as the town coroner, assessor, school committee member and selectman, as well as handling the job of commissioner of wrecks for Plymouth County.

As town representative to the state in the early 1840s, he helped to create a Hull legend. Hull in those days usually enrolled fewer than fifty voters, and most of them worked as lighters and fishermen, sometimes spending days at a time on the sea. Others toiled on offshore islands, or kept the lamps burning at Boston Lighthouse. In November 1842, the state's gubernatorial election came down to a deadlock, with only Hull not reporting in. The town's fishermen came in to shore, visited the polls, and Representative Tower headed to Boston to cast the deciding vote for Marcus Morton as governor of Massachusetts. From that day, the town became a political barometer for the state, the townsfolk proudly living by the motto, "As Hull goes, so goes the state."

As a man of the sea, Tower could not help but become involved in matters pertaining to ships passing up and down the Nantasket peninsula, and traversing in and out of Boston Harbor. Due to the strategic location of the town's headlands at the mouth of the harbor, they became prime communication points for the merchants of the city. Prior to the invention of the telegraph, word traveled by means of signal flags from point to point across the harbor. Merchants awaiting the arrival of ships used the early warnings to dispatch wharfingers to the waterfront in anticipation of efficiently and cost-effectively unloading cargo. But the system could fail during foggy weather when, if messages got through at all, they could be misinterpreted between Hull's Souther's Hill and Long Island. Tower helped to modernize the system, laying one of the first telegraph lines in the country from Hull's newly-named Telegraph Hill to the Chamber of Commerce in Boston.

Some of Tower's greatest accomplishments, though, came in connection with the Humane Society. In 1840, Tower had been chosen as the first keeper of the society's lifeboat in Hull, leading to the heroic events of the night of December 17, 1841 and the rescue of the crew of the *Mohawk*. The satisfaction of that moment, though, did not force Tower into complacency. On the lookout for the next shipwreck, which, at that time, was inevitable, Tower petitioned the

Humane Society for more equipment. In the minutes of the meeting of the Society's Trustees held on January 3, 1845, the subject of the lifeboat requested by Tower and Captain Josiah Sturgis was referred to Charles Amory, Samuel Austin and Robert Bennett Forbes. According to Homer,

> At the suggestion of Capt. Sturgis and Mr. Tower, the Humane Society have recently erected a new boat house on the north side of Stony beach, near Point Alderton, in which there is an elegant, substantial, copper-fastened life-boat, of extensive dimensions. I should think it capable of holding thirty or forty persons, besides her 'gallant crew.' She is calculated for eight oars. This boat was much wanted. There are now two excellent boats there, one of which is on the northeast side, besides two 'humane houses,' for the accommodation of shipwrecked seamen. The people of Hull are now better prepared to render assistance to wrecked vessels and their crew than they ever were before.

While the first boat placed in 1840 guarded the three and a half mile sandy stretch of beach from Point Allerton to Atlantic Hill, the new boat protected the northern shore of the peninsula, opposite Boston Light, the area where ships entering or already in Boston Harbor that were then attacked by northerly winds were likely to come ashore. Moreover, according to the minutes of the January 3, 1845, meeting, "Mr. [Daniel] Parker, chairman of the committee appointed for the purpose, reported that a contract had been made for one dozen Life-Preservers, for the crew of the boat at Hull."

Prominently positioned as they were, the Hull fishermen of the 1840s had an unparalleled vantage point from which to watch and critique the state of the mercantile world, or at least that part of it that pertained to wood, canvas, hemp and sextants. It was in their front yards, in many cases, that ships ended up, either run aground intact, or floated ashore in pieces and collected as salvage. With shipwrecks increasing in frequency as the decade progressed, the local captains called an "indignation meeting," with the support of their selectmen, planning to express their feelings on the subject to the marine insurance underwriters of Boston. Homer published their meeting minutes as an appendix to his *Notes on the Sea-Shore*:

> Whereas, the quiet, industrious citizens of Hull have noticed, with regret and indignation, but with the feelings of men and of christians, as they humbly trust, the rapid increase of shipwrecks, and of accidents to our mercantile marine, on Nantasket Beach, the Hardings, Cohasset rocks, at Marshfield, Scituate, and other places at that vicinity; And, whereas, those that have occurred of late are believed to have been caused, for the most part, through the ignorance, inexperience, carelessness, or want of proper attention and skill on the part of those in command of the vessels which have been partially or wholly wrecked - in some instances involving the loss of valuable human lives as well as property; And, whereas, of late years we have been shocked at the frequent midnight calls made upon us to proceed to Long-Beach and its neighborhood, to save the fragments of wrecks and the lives of mariners; And, whereas, there is reason to believe that many of the youthful captains sailing out of Boston are unfitted for the business they are engaged in, either from a want of experience as seamen, sound judgment and skill as navigators, or the absence of a proper alacrity, when approaching the coast, and who are too often put in command of vessels through the undue influence of wealthy relatives; And, whereas these things are becoming highly offensive to the unpretending, hard-fisted citizens of Hull and of Hingham, some of whom have followed fishing twenty-five and thirty years, without running ashore, or without meeting with a single accident; Therefore...

What followed was a list or resolves, some tongue-in-cheek, but all grounded in the real perceptions of the local mariners.

> Resolved, That there are four points to the compass, N.E.S.W.; and any captain of a vessel who cannot box the compass, deserves to have his ears boxed.
>
> Resolved, That an education received by rubbing against the walls of a college, or passing through its halls, is not so serviceable to a sea-captain as one received upon the Ocean, amidst high winds, heavy seas, and hard knocks.
>
> Resolved, That maps and charts are useful to navigators at sea, and he who neglects to study them thoroughly is a blockhead of the first class, and ought not to be entrusted with the command of a first class ship.
>
> Resolved, That the beach at Marshfield is not Boston Light House, 'any way you can fix it.'
>
> Resolved, As the deliberate opinion of this meeting, that when a sea-captain, when approaching our coast, his course due W., finds himself getting rapidly into shoal water, the safest way is to wear ship, and run to the Eastward, instead of running plump onto the beach or the rocks.

Tower, with the only hotel in the village, was perhaps more attuned to the miseries of shipwreck victims than the others. For, when the lifeboats returned to shore, the local lifesavers transported the troubled seamen directly into the hands of Tower and his wife. Together they fed them, clothed them, listened to their tales of woe, and, when they were ready, sent them on their way.

During his years in Hull, Tower became a close friend of Joshua James, the man who would become known as the greatest lifesaver in American history. Although Tower would leave town in 1856, their bond would remain for almost another half century. The

Hull Beacon reported on April 23, 1898, that "Captain Moses B. Tower has presented Captain Joshua James, of the lifesaving station, a beautifully ornamented swordfish-sword, which is about twenty-eight inches in length." It was a gift of the sea, from one of her own to another.

In November of 1856, Tower and his family moved to East Boston, purchasing the Samuel Hall house. He continued in the fishing industry, owning a fleet of ships (the *William Daisley*, *Olive G. Tower*, and *Mary B. Tower*) that hauled in mackerel in the summer and sailed to Jamaica in the winter time to take part in the banana trade. He also worked as a submarine contractor and wreckmaster of Boston Harbor, excelling at both floating ships that had been stranded and raising from the depths anything that may have been salvageable from the harbor's many shipping disasters.

While in Boston, he also spent time as the director of that city's branch of the Pacific National Bank and signed up as an active member of the Boston Marine Society. In 1879, the family moved again, this time inland to Auburndale. Although it was here that he would spend the remaining years of his life, he never forgot Hull. He even joined the fledgling Hull Yacht Club in September of 1881. Seven years later he retired from active business.

With all of these achievements, Tower's crowning moment may have come on October 7, 1844. Discovering a brig smashing ashore on the Point Allerton bar, Tower secured the assistance of William James and his own brother, John Wesley Tower. Together, with Moses' horses, they retrieved the lifeboat from the Stony Beach boathouse, the boat for which Moses had lobbied the Humane Society. As they headed for a proper launch site, about a mile and a half away, Captain Tower recruited five more men for the rescue attempt. All eight entered the boat, with Tower on the sweep oar. Through tempestuous conditions they pulled, over cresting waves, for a full mile.

Captain Leeds of the brig *Tremont* of New York had been quarantined to the quarterdeck with his officers and crew for seven heart-pounding hours. Their eyes widened and hope sparked anew as the small lifeboat bounded over the waves, defying Neptune's deadly demands. Within moments, the lifeboat pulled alongside the brig and the rescuers pulled the exhausted victims from the jaws of death.

According to the *Boston Daily Advertiser and Patriot* of October 14, 1844, "Captain Leeds gratefully declares, that he owes his own life, and the lives of his crew, under the blessing of Divine Providence, to the exertions they generously made in their behalf. He has made a communication of the case to the Trustees of the Humane Society; and we are confident that it will receive the consideration which it so obviously merits."

The Trustees did take notice. Later that year they awarded "Moses B. Tower, John W. Tower, William James, and five others, for their humane and heroic exertions in saving, by the Life-Boat of the Society, stationed at Hull, the officers and crew of the brig Tremont, of New York, wrecked on Point Alderton Bar, in a violent gale, on Monday, Oct. 7, ten dollars in money to each, together with the Society's Gold Medal, to Capt. Tower, in token of the approbation of the Trustees of his and their meritorious conduct."

In 1843, the Trustees awarded six dollars to Captain Isaiah Harding and four dollars to each of his six crew members for attempting to rescue the sailors of the brig *President* through the use of the Humane Society's lifeboat at Chatham. But there was no rescue, as no lives were saved, despite the strenuous attempt. Moses Tower, therefore, in the aftermath of the *Tremont* incident, became the first coxswain in command of a Humane Society lifeboat to receive the society's coveted gold medal.

"This is the third instance in which this boat, stationed at Hull, has been the means of preserving life," stated the *Daily Advertiser and Patriot*. "The first was that of the crew of the *Emeline*, from which five men were saved; the second that of the *Mohawk*, when twelve were saved, and thirdly, this of the *Tremont*, as just related. Had the Legislature of Massachusetts made provision only for this single boat, such results would alone have sufficiently attested the wisdom and humanity of the appropriation." In two months' time, the Hull crew would add yet another rescue to their tally, that of the crew of the ship *Massasoit*. On a first attempt to reach the vessel, the crew was thwarted by high seas. On a second attempt, they succeeded in rescuing twelve of the thirteen people aboard. One man had sought refuge in the hold and was believed drowned. He emerged, though, after the lifeboat had departed and was spotted by a local pilot boat, which headed to his aid. Tragically, the aft section of the ship, on which he was standing, gave way before the pilots could reach him, and he succumbed to the waves.

Moses Binney Tower passed away on November 28, 1898, two days after the devastating Portland Gale had claimed approximately five hundred lives between New Jersey and Nova Scotia. His death could not have come at a worse time for his Hull friends. Joshua James, caring for survivors, assessing damage, and identifying bodies after rescuing twenty men from four ships over two days, could not get to Auburndale for the funeral, and so never had a chance to say good-bye. Tower's body was transported to Hingham, the town of his birth, for interment with full Masonic honors. And Moses Tower, self-made, active man, was buried as the first decorated Humane Society lifeboat hero.

Chapter 10:
Onto the National Scene

By 1845, the Humane Society's lifeboat roster included eighteen individual craft. And, according to the 1845 *History of the Humane Society of Massachusetts*, the idea of huts of refuge, though sixty years old, still had merit. "At an early period of the Society," it states, "the erection of huts for the shelter and comfort of persons unfortunately shipwrecked was among the objects of its attention. Within a few months after its organization appropriations were made for this purpose. Several huts, on exposed parts of the Massachusetts coast, have been from time to time erected, repaired or renewed, as circumstances required, furnished with fuel and other articles most needful for the exhausted mariner. At no time have the trustees lost sight of this object..."

If, though, they had never lost faith in the idea, they certainly had tempered their enthusiasm for building the huts, redirecting their energy towards the lifeboat stations. In 1845, the shrunken list of active huts reflected the fact that the Massachusetts population was growing, and rapidly. In 1790, just a few short years after the Society had formed, 378,787 people called the state home. By 1840, that number had nearly doubled, to 737,699. By 1850, it would be 994,514. The lonely Massachusetts coast of 1790 was not so remote in 1845. The dozen or so huts left stood on Tinker's Island in Marblehead, and on Great Brewster and Lovell's Island in Boston Harbor; on the still unsettled strip of sand at Nantasket, on the

During Massachusetts Governor George N. Briggs's administration the state appropriated $2500 to build three more lifeboats to be placed along the coast.

Scituate shore and on Duxbury's "Long Beach"; on the Cape at Race Point, Nauset Beach and off Chatham; and "At Nantucket, also, there are several huts, under the charge of individuals of that island."

The state Legislature continued its support of the Society into the 1850s. In the Acts of 1849, the state, under Governor George Nixon Briggs, appropriated $2500 for the construction and placement of three more lifeboats, for "the southern part of Plumb Island, one at Wellfleet, and one at Provincetown, near Race Point." In a continuation of the practice begun by the Society with the Hull crew in 1845, the "Resolve for the Preservation of Human Life" expanded to include "for the crews of all the life-boats stationed on the coast, suitable life-preservers." Another major transition had taken place. The Society had begun to paternalistically oversee the safety of the lifeboat crews, understanding that without healthy and willing crews, the lifeboats themselves were useless. In 1852, the state set aside $2500 for repair and maintenance costs for the lifeboat fleet.

In 1854, the state passed the first in a series of acts intended to "Protect the Property of the Humane Society of Massachusetts." As noted in the 1845 *History*, the vandalism that plagued the Society's earliest efforts continued into the middle of the nineteenth century. "We regret for the sake of our common humanity to be compelled to say, that neither the sacredness of the charity, nor the urgent necessity to the shipwrecked sufferers of the materials supplied; nor yet the thought of the bitter disappointment and distress, which the want of them at such a crisis much occasion, have protected these humble but hallowed abodes from plunder." To combat the sabotage of the huts, the state made it illegal to enter a Humane Society building and "willfully injure, destroy, remove or carry away, any food, fuel, oil, candles, furniture, utensils or other property belonging to said society" and, in the case of the lifeboat stations, "carry away, remove or injure, any life-boat, car, or any of the ropes, tackle, oars, or any appurtenance thereof, or willfully injure or destroy, or unlawfully use or commit any trespass upon, the property of said society." Fines could reach $100, and the jail term could be as high as ninety days for the misdemeanor offense.

Until 1848, the story of organized lifesaving of mariners in distress at sea in American waters could mostly be told from a singular perspective, that of the Massachusetts shore. But by the early 1840s, the federal government of the United States had taken several steps toward increasing the safety of seagoing travel and cargo transport. The first colonial lighthouse constructed in the New World, Boston Light, shined forth from Little Brewster Island, north of Hull, in 1716. By 1820, fifty-five lighthouses lined the Atlantic coast, coordinated by the federal government since 1789. The formation of the Revenue Cutter Service on August 4, 1790, showed that the United States would vigorously fight for tax revenues due the young country; in 1832, Congress expanded that organization's duties to include patrolling the East Coast during the winter to aid ships in danger of going ashore, becoming inextricably entangled in ice floes, or potentially facing myriad other problems associated with being at sea during the coldest months of the year. The fourth revenue cutter, the *Massachusetts*, launched from Newburyport on July 15, 1791, captained by John Foster Williams, a member of the Boston Marine

Society. The sloop served for just fifteen months before being sold, and replaced the following spring by the *Massachusetts II*. Various other vessels followed.

Also in 1807, the federal government directed that a systematic survey of the coast be implemented, providing mariners a fighting chance against the abundant but hidden shoals and ledges that lurked close to shore in relatively shallow water. And in 1838, the United States began methodically providing inspections for steamboats and their engines. "There is no doubt," wrote Robert F. Bennett in *Surfboats, Rockets and Carronades*, "that each of these...steps to prevent shipwrecks and disaster contributed substantially to the improvement in safety, and had they not existed, countless additional lives would have been lost on the coasts of this new nation in the first 60 years of its existence." In Massachusetts, sailors that slipped past all of these safeguards and still wrecked their ships could find their way to safety either under their own power in huts of refuge, or could be rescued by volunteer lifesavers heading out in small boats at their own peril. Elsewhere in the United States, though, that final, important piece of the lifesaving network had not been put in place.

The idea of providing a fleet of vessels for the potential rescue of sailors in peril did not begin with the Humane Society of the Commonwealth of Massachusetts. Chinese lifeboats had been placed on the Yangtze River in the Middle Ages. According to Clayton D. Evans in "Towards a Humanitarian Ideal" in *Wreck & Rescue Journal*,

> In Portugal as early as 1691, King D. Pedro II had issued an edict that the Masters of all coastal forts make every effort to render aid to those shipwrecked within their immediate scope of influence. In Great Britain, a permanent charitable trust had been established in 1751, not far from Tynemouth at Bamburgh Castle, its principal goal being the salvation of those shipwrecked in the area. In 1769, an effort was made in The Netherlands to extend humanitarian relief from shore to sea when a series of rescue boats were proposed for the West Frisian Islands.

Eventually, the humanitarian ideals espoused by the national lifesaving societies would find common ground with more localized interests, particularly of a commercial nature, and Humane Societies would begin to appear at specific ports or geographic areas. These societies were centered around major trading zones such as Liverpool, Dublin, Oporto, Seville and Boulougne. A great deal of the incentive for creating these organizations came from parties with vested interests in saving ships, cargoes and seafarers (most probably in that order), namely ship-owners and underwriters. In 1802, in fact, Lloyd's of London established the first 'life-boat fund' with the aim of establishing lifeboats at strategic locations all along the coasts of the United Kingdom. It would be these local humane societies which would extend the lifesaving concept in Europe and the New World beyond the mere provision of assistance to those fortunate enough to make it ashore, to that of providing waterborne rescue with the use of dedicated lifeboats and crews. The original humane societies and later the lifeboat services would become, in many countries, the first secular charities and their cause would, eventually, appeal to a broad spectrum of national society soliciting donations from both the upper echelons of the populace as well as the common man.

In 1824, Great Britain and the Netherlands formed their national lifesaving services, with Portugal, Spain and Prussia following soon thereafter. The Belgian Lifesaving Service, the first successful government-funded lifeboat service, founded in 1838, still operates today.

Evans' contention that the creation of lifeboat societies around the world were fostered by desires to save "ships, cargoes and seafarers (most probably in that order)," while sounding callous towards humanity in general, is solid. While human life was important, what governments and owners of mercantile interests truly needed most was that safe delivery of cargo. The Humane Society of the Commonwealth of Massachusetts bucked that trend, forming for exactly the opposite purpose, but for the United States at large, economic needs ruled the day.

The unprotected nature of the New Jersey shoreline in particular had garnered attention from that state's government. A horrific February 1846 storm drove nine ships ashore on thirty-five miles of coast on the approach to New York Harbor, and outcries against supposed looting and illegal salvaging reached the ears of the state legislature. "As a consequence," wrote Robert F. Bennett in *Surfboats, Rockets and Carronades*, "an investigatory commission was appointed by the Legislature of the State of New Jersey. The report of that commission, dated March 1846, revealed that of those nine vessels, efforts to assist were made in each case by the inhabitants of the coast. Their aid resulted in the saving of 64 lives of the 110 imperiled."

Prior to the February 1846 disasters, the federal government had made one little-remembered attempt at establishing a life-saving service on the shores of the United States. A heartrending tale of loss unfolded on January 2, 1837 when the bark *Mexico* wrecked on a shoal off Hempstead Beach, Long Island, New York. Driven to the ship's exposed deck when the decks below flooded, one hundred and twenty-four passengers and crew stood trembling from fear, exhaustion and freezing temperatures as local residents ashore built a bonfire and gathered the courage to help the strangers in danger of dying just offshore. One man, Raynor Rock Smith, hauled out a small boat and called for a volunteer crew. Men responded, and together they rowed to the ship and back, bringing seven men and a boy back alive.

"The landing of the eight men from the wreck," wrote John R. Spears in the *New York Times* in 1904,

> ...had brought forth a rousing cheer from the people along shore and from those on the wreck as well. It was the only cry of pleasure heard on the wreck. When no one responded to Smith's appeals for a

second crew the silent refusal was seen by the eager watchers on the wreck, and the cheers they had given were turned to cries and shrieks of despair. And these wailing cries, with prayers for help, continued into the night until one by one they were hushed in death.

When the storm had ceased and the wreck was boarded, the deck was found covered with bodies that glistened in the sunlight because they were coated with ice. Mothers were sitting crouched over their children in a vain effort to ward from them the stinging spray, and the girls lay with their arms around each other. A few over sixty bodies were recovered, and of these sixty-two were buried in the cemetery at Rockville Centre, where a monument, erected to perpetuate their memory can still be seen, with its quaint inscription.

The Treasury Department now hired its lighthouse keepers with their ability to potentially save people in the surf in mind. Raynor Rock Smith received an appointment to the keeper's job at Fire Island Light on Long Island. Furthermore, the government sent U.S. Navy Lieutenant William D. Porter, son of Commodore David Porter and brother of Admiral David Dixon Porter, and then tasked with overseeing the lighthouses from New York to Virginia, to Europe to study lighthouses and other lifesaving appliances. He returned speaking in favor of placing lifeboats at lighthouses themselves.

The topic vanished from national discussion for seven years. In 1845, the Secretary of the Treasury sent the team of Navy Lieutenants Thornton A. Jenkins and Richard Bache to Great Britain, France and Belgium to study lighthouses. In August 1846 they submitted their report, which commented extraneously on the presence of a number of lifeboats at Liverpool. They recommended that a similar system be adopted in the United States. Congressman Robert McClelland of Michigan, Chairman of the House Committee on Commerce on February 25, 1847, moved to appropriate $5,000 for the placement of lifesaving equipment at Atlantic coast lighthouses. On March 4, 1847, Congress passed legislation appropriating the

Congressman William Augustus Newell of New Jersey brought attention to the need for more lifeboats nationally after witnessing a wreck on the shores of his home state in 1839.

funds "furnishing the lighthouses or other exposed places where vessels are liable to be driven on shore, with boats or other suitable means of assistance." But the appropriation was never acted upon, and the money remained in federal coffers.

The following year a freshman congressman from New Jersey, Dr. William Augustus Newell, asked that the House Committee on Commerce investigate what could be done to improve the chances of sailors surviving shipwrecks on American shores. Garnering no response from his peers, Newell wrote an impassioned speech in anticipation of adding an amendment to an impending lighthouse appropriation bill. While working as a doctor in Manahawkin, Newell had witnessed the devastation of a shipwreck firsthand on August 13, 1839 when the Austrian brig *Terasto* wrecked on a shoal off New Jersey's then-uninhabited Long Beach Island. Thirteen men drowned before his eyes.

On August 3, 1848, Newell delivered his speech, apparently catching the attention of his peers by offering them the staggering statistics that between April 12, 1839 and July 31, 1848 at least 338 vessels had wrecked along the shores of New Jersey and New York – 68 full-rigged ships, 88 brigs, 30 barks, 140 schooners and 12 sloops - and that from February 1846 to July 1848 alone, 122 of those ships had wrecked. On August 9, his proposed amendment to the bill, "for providing surfboats, rockets, carronades, and other necessary apparatus for the better protection of life and property from shipwrecks on the coast of New Jersey, between Sandy Hook and Little Egg Harbor, ten thousand dollars; the same to be expended under the supervision of such officers of the Revenue Marine Corps as may be detached for this duty by the Secretary of the Treasury" was attached. Congress "eagerly anticipating adjournment, seized upon such an opportunity to avoid dissenting argument over such an innocuous piece of legislation," wrote Bennett, voted it through unanimously. As such, the United States Life-Saving Service was born a few days later, on August 14.

Although the argument could be made that there never was an inappropriate time to begin a federal lifesaving system along American shores, the timing of the Act of August 14, 1848 proved to be especially providential, and particularly so for the approach to New York Harbor. Human tragedy overseas was about to change the American landscape forever. "The famine in Ireland caused a large migration into the port of New York around 1847-1851," wrote Van Field in *Wrecks and Rescues on Long Island*. "Large numbers of ships loaded with human cargo were arriving. Passenger rates were lower in winter so the poor were more likely to arrive during the worst weather." Approximately one million Irish men, women and children died during the famine, and one million more emigrated, most heading to the United States. Boston would see its share of similar tragedies. On Sunday, October 17, 1849, the brig *St. John*, a famine ship from Galway, struck on rocks off the Cohasset shore, leaving ninety-nine dead. The local Humane Society crew launched to save the crew of the British ship wrecking at the town harbor's mouth, but was too late to save the immigrants of the *St. John*.

The Trustees of the Humane Society did not sit idly by while Congress took their actions to initiate a lifesaving system for the port of New York. They felt that given their historic efforts, the state of Massachusetts deserved as much federal underwriting as any other state. On September 25, 1848, a month after the $10,000 appropriation, the Society petitioned Secretary of Treasury Robert J. Walker for a portion of the funds, via a letter signed by Trustees

Abbott Lawrence and Robert Bennett Forbes. After determining that the funds dedicated to the New Jersey shore would indeed be used appropriately, Walker informed the Society that instead of receiving funds from that appropriation, the Society would be given the $5,000 appropriated under the Lighthouse Act in 1847. On October 17, the society acknowledged receipt of the funds through the Collector of Customs for the port of Boston.

Thus began the relationship between the Humane Society of the Commonwealth of Massachusetts and what would become the United States Life-Saving Service. Six decades of work on the Massachusetts shore had finally been validated by the rest of the country. The Humane Society had reached the national stage, but there was plenty of work to be done. At this critical point in its history, the Society allowed a dynamic, progressive member of the board of Trustees utilize his technical expertise and vision to shape the future of its lifesaving operations.

Chapter 11:
Dedicated to the Cause

R obert Bennett Forbes was born in the Jamaica Plain section of Roxbury on September 18, 1804, destined to a life on the sea. The son of Ralph Bennett Forbes and Margaret Perkins, young Robert learned at the knee of his successful uncle Thomas Handasyd Perkins. Thomas had helped initiate the Canton trade, sailing overseas in 1789. In 1815, when Robert was just ten years old, Thomas and his brother James Perkins opened a trading house on the Mediterranean in order to begin buying Turkish opium for resale in China. Robert had witnessed firsthand the great amount of wealth derivable from the life of a merchant.

Forbes' first journey upon the sea came when he was just six years old, joining his mother on the *Midas* to France in 1811, to be with his father. The return voyage in 1813 was probably more impacting on his future life, as the family, now numbering four with the arrival of baby brother John Murray Forbes, was forced to run a British blockade to reach Baltimore. "Shipping before the mast on the *Canton Packet* in 1813," wrote Samuel Eliot Morison in *The Maritime History of Massachusetts, 1783-1860*, "'with a capital consisting of a Testament, a Bowditch, a quadrant, a chest of sea clothes and a mother's blessing,' he rose to be a master at twenty, passed but six months ashore in ten years of China trading, and commanded his own ship at twenty-six." Competent of the needs of his fellow seamen

Captain Robert Bennett Forbes proved to be a giant in the history of the Humane Society, an unshakeable force for the forward momentum of the organization (Courtesy of the Robert Bennett Forbes House Museum).

from the state of Massachusetts, Forbes joined the Boston Marine Society in 1824.

During these years of the vigorousness of youth, Forbes paused to observe the charitable actions of his uncles. In the second decade of the nineteenth century, when the movement arose for the establishment of a Massachusetts General Hospital, James and Thomas Handasyd Perkins each contributed $5,000 to the creation of its endowment, "which of course represented in 1816 what a far larger benefaction would mean today," wrote Mark Anthony DeWolfe Howe in *The Humane Society of the Commonwealth of Massachusetts* in 1918. Later, in 1826, the brothers gave several thousands more for an addition to the Boston Athenaeum. In 1832, to help the faltering Massachusetts Asylum for the Blind Thomas donated his mansion on Pearl Street in Boston for use as its home. In 1839, he sold that mansion and gave the school the funds for a third, larger home. Both brothers joined as members of the Humane Society. Forbes pocketed these memories and continued his ascendency in the mercantile world.

At twenty-eight years old Forbes joined the firm of Russell & Company in China, and before a decade was out he was at its head. Back in Boston in 1840, according to Morison, he "engaged in various picturesque and benevolent side activities. An early convert to the screw-propeller and the iron steamer, he would have had Massachusetts lead in steam as in sail; he did introduce auxiliary steamers to the waters of China, and built the first ocean-going twin-screw iron tugboat, which was appropriately named *R.B. Forbes*." In 1841, at thirty-seven years old, he was selected as a Trustee of the Humane Society. His most famous days were still ahead.

In 1846, when news of the famine in Ireland sent shockwaves of grief and concern throughout the northeast, the merchants of Boston moved quickly to alleviate the suffering. Mayor Josiah Quincy, Jr., was chosen to head the New England Relief Committee for the Famine in Ireland and Scotland. "Through free advertising and local commissions," wrote Morison, "cash and provisions to the value of over $150,000 (of which $115,500 [came] from Massachusetts) were quickly collected in New England, and a few hundred dollars additional came in from Yankees in the West, all forwarded to the wharves free of transportation charges." Even the vessels to be used to deliver the goods came free of charge.

The merchants of the city called out to one of their own, U.S. Representative Robert Charles Winthrop, petitioning him on February 22, 1847, to secure Navy ships from Congress for the transport of the goods and cash. With the Mexican War grabbing most of the attention of the country's lawmakers, the idea was approved, and Congress sent the frigate *Macedonian* to New York and the sloop of war *Jamestown* to Boston. Rather than assigning them to the state's governments, they were loaned to specific men who would be responsible for them. Robert Bennett Forbes took command of the *Jamestown*. Commodore F.A. Parker, commanding the Charlestown Navy Yard, stripped the vessel of its guns and delivered the vessel to Forbes. According to Forbes' own account, *The Voyage of the Jamestown on Her Errand of Mercy*, on March 17, "being St. Patrick's Day, the 'Laborer's Aid Society,' of Boston, composed principally, if not entirely, of poor Irishmen, put their hands and minds to the holy work, and in the course of that day, one-seventh part of the cargo was stowed away." Eleven days later, the tug *R.B. Forbes* pulled the sloop away from the city, and at 3 p.m. on the 28th, the *Jamestown* cleared the Truro Highlands and sailed for the British Isles. Fifteen days later, she dropped anchor off Cork. Forbes, acting on behalf of the charitable people of Boston, received the thanks of a nation. He did not linger, though invitations to do so came thick and fast. Instead, he raced home to help load and deliver the final three quarters of the goods collected for the cause.

Two years later, Forbes again made headlines. On June 27, 1849, seven hundred miles west of Cape Clear, off the Irish coast, the Cunard side-wheel steamer *Europa* ran down the bark *Charles Bartlett* of Plymouth, Massachusetts, in a heavy fog, sinking her and her load of Irish emigrants in about three minutes. "The scene during those few minutes was appalling in the extreme," wrote the *Liverpool Times*. "A crowd of suffering passengers, maimed and broken by the collision, lay dead or dying at the spot where the bows of the Europa had entered. Some of the individuals who had entered the deck appeared panic-stricken, others ran shrieking to and fro in despair, while some rushed forward and eagerly seized upon the opportunities which were presented for giving them a chance of safety." Standing aboard the *Europa* and seeing people in danger of succumbing to the waves, Forbes moved decisively. He leaped from the steamer into the water, and, according to Morison, "he passed the end of a rope around a fat German, and clung to him while both were alternately jerked out of the water and plunged under it by the rolling of the ship to which the rope was fast." When that man was found to be dead, Forbes took to an oar on one of the *Europa*'s lifeboats and helped pull survivors from the ocean. Of the 162 people aboard the *Charles Bartlett*, only forty-three lived to tell of the tragedy.

The captain of the *Europa*, William Bartlett, watched in amazement. "I particularly observed one passenger using the most noble exertions; I saw him let himself overboard, and clench a man in his arms, and, finding him dead, let him go. I next saw him on the bow of a boat, hauling a man from under water with a boat hook, who was afterwards restored to life on board. I afterwards found that person to be R.B. Forbes, of Boston." Lloyd's Shipwreck Society of London presented Forbes with a medal for his heroism, as did the Liverpool Shipwreck and Humane Society. The praise did not end there.

That you were a passenger on the steamer *Europa* on her voyage to Europe has brought the calamity that occurred very near to us. We have noticed that the exposure of your own life to save the lives of others, on that dreadful occasion, has attracted the attention and admiration of several humane institutions in the Kingdom of Great Britain, and that you have been presented with their escutcheons. As that occurrence took place on the high seas - on the broad ocean - it is the subject of the care and admiration of the Massachusetts Humane Society, equally with the societies of Great Britain. Useful and various have been the passages of your life; none have been more stirring than this: -

"It is no act of common passage, but a strain of rareness."

Herewith you will receive the Society's medal, presented to you for your manly efforts to save life in this sudden and overwhelming disaster on the wide ocean."

We recollect for many years your active philanthropy, your zeal for the mariner, and your high character as a merchant. Very often we are reminded of your absence by the want of your services. We trust that prosperity and health await you, and that you will be safely returned, long to continue your useful destiny among us.

Accept our high esteem and warm regard, and sincere desire for your return to us.

By order of the trustees of the Massachusetts Humane Society.

E.H. Robbins

Francis Parkman

Daniel P. Parker

Committee

The man that was charged with determining the worthiness of potential lifesaving medal recipients had himself become a lifesaving hero. The two gold medals the Society awarded in 1849 - to Forbes and Captain Mulford Rich of Wellfleet - were the last they gave out until 1880, as they switched to silver medals as their top awards the following year.

Forbes' usefulness to the Humane Society stretched beyond his fame, worldly connections and thoughtfulness on the wants of the American sailor. "Robert Bennet Forbes," said Morison, "had the most original brain, and the most attractive personality of any Boston merchant of his generation." As reflected in his promotion of the steam vessel, Forbes had a knack for understanding and evaluating the potential of new technologies. He used this skill to great reward on behalf of the society, and, ultimately, the United States Life-Saving Service. After the Congressional appropriation of 1848 was awarded to the New York Board of Underwriters, their president, Walter Jones, made it his first order of business to contact Forbes for his advice on lifesaving equipment. "Thereupon," wrote Bennett, "on November 18 Mr. Forbes forwarded a printed instruction to the Secretary of the Treasury on the methods and equipment in use by his Society. It is obvious that this data was instrumental in guiding the New York Underwriters when they put together their plans for a national service."

Among the many books and pamphlets which Forbes would write in his lifetime, the most beneficial to the country's lifesavers was his *Lifeboats, projectiles and other means for saving life*, compiled in

1872. Its pages illustrate the deliberate contemplation Forbes had put into the subject for many years. They also show his complete confidence and conviction of his opinions.

In 1855, the Humane Society received six metallic lifeboats from the federal government, designed by Boston native Joseph Francis at his Greenport, New York, Novelty Iron Works. While Francis' metal life-car had proved its worth in the Ayrshire rescue off New Jersey in 1849, Francis' metallic lifeboat left much to desire in the eyes of Forbes:

> It has long been the opinion of our surf men that the metallic lifeboats placed by the Government on the coast of New Jersey, and those given to the Massachusetts Humane Society by the same, are practically valueless as surf-boats. The Humane Society were very glad to receive and house these boats at the time, thinking there might be cases where ships with emigrants might find them useful. The Society have six situated at the following points; Nantucket Bar, Monomoy, Chatham, Nausett, Gloucester, Scituate, they were handed over to the Society by the Secretary of the Treasury, June 5, 1855, since that time, so far as I remember, their record of services stands thus: Nantucket once manned in a comparatively smooth time, and found to pull well; Monomoy boat was made use of to take the crew off a vessel about 15 years ago, and having no rough water did the work well; Chatham boat has never been distinguished in saving life; Nausett has been afloat two or three times, once in very cold weather within a year or two, but the wind was off shore, the sea not rough, the seaman say that they would not have attempted to go off in her had it been rough; the Scituate boat has never been utilized in saving life; the Gloucester boat has been made useful on several occasions in boarding wrecks in comparatively

smooth water, pulling out of the harbor, but has never been subjected to a severe trial."

While he responded negatively to the Francis boat as a surf-launched craft, Forbes suggested that the metallic lifeboats could be well utilized as shipboard lifeboats, noting that their durability was outstanding, especially in comparison to wooden boats.

Aside from lifeboats, Forbes watched over the development of line-throwing gun technology with an eye towards its implementation on the Massachusetts shore. The notion of fixing a line to a projectile and firing it from a shore-based gun to a ship in distress struck Sergeant John Bell of the Royal Artillery in 1789, and two years later he offered a demonstration to that effect with a mortar. Captain George Manby, another Englishman, designed his own mortar in 1807, saving lives with it two years later. The line delivered by the Manby mortar extended from the Yarmouth shore to the brig *Nancy* and created a rope bridge local boatmen could use to pull themselves out to the ship. Colonel R.A. Boxer experimented with rockets as a delivery vehicle in the 1850s and 1860s.

Delivering a line to a ship was a logical first step in the evolution of the practice of rescuing mariners from shipwrecks without the use of a boat. While in the early days, as exemplified by Manby, the use of a line as a guide to a ship for a lifeboat proved successful, one major drawback to this plan would normally make it a second choice. Theoretically, the most dangerous moment of a rescue attempt for a boat launched from shore comes in the first few seconds. Breaking waves crashing the shore expend their energy there and then. A surfboat crew (surfboats were usually shorter and lighter than lifeboats) had to fight up, over and even through the surf, often becoming soaking wet by the freezing cold water in the act. Once clearing the breakers, while it was still a dangerous endeavor, the pull to the shipwreck could be anticlimactic. Returning to the beach could also be onerous, but not necessarily as tough as the initial plunge.

With surf as the main enemy of the lifesavers, a ship stuck within the breaking waves caused special problems. Retrieving freezing and near-death sailors from a shipwreck was in itself a precarious task; trying to do so as waves were breaking over both vessels could be impossible. An established rope bridge offered opportunities to avoid such situations.

A heavy line, or hawser, connected from the mast of a ship to an anchor of some sort on the land - most commonly a large wooden cross buried in the sand and known as a sand anchor - could be added onto. Sailors could pull on the hawser and drag items affixed to it to the ship. A pulley, or block, tied to the mast below the hawser, allowed for the establishment of a movable continuous loop of line when that line was run through a matching block on shore. With both ends of that line made fast to a ring, anything could be hung from the line.

In 1832, Lieutenant Thomas Kisbee, Royal Navy, designed an improvement to his "Kisbee ring," known today by the more common name "life ring." Sewing canvas around the ring, Kisbee opened a world of possibilities. He attached a pair of canvas pants, or breeches, to the life ring and hung them from a traveling block that rested its weight on the hawser, but was movable by means of the whip. "The breeches buoy was easily suspended from a line, the survivor could not fall out or be dashed against the side of the wreck and even better, it floated, for in many cases, although a person might have been suspended by the life-line, they were not necessarily clear of the sea," writes Clayton Evans in *Rescue at Sea*. According to Forbes, early uses in Massachusetts, specifically on Nantucket, included "A simple bowline hung to a snatch block, to travel by means of the whip or hauling line." He added, though, that "Recently we have adopted the Beechings cork body buoy with canvas legs, to be hung to the traveling rope by a bridle." The version of the breeches buoy used by the Humane Society can be traced to Great Yarmouth in England, and lifeboat builder James Beeching.

Where plausible, and if sea or weather conditions warranted removing multiple sailors at once, the Humane Society used the Francis metallic life-car, an enclosed, nearly egg-shaped pod that could be attached to the beach apparatus lines in similar fashion to the breeches buoy. Forbes, though, had concerns about them, noting their weight - 400 to 500 pounds - as a major barrier to their frequent use.

Forbes' diligence in the study of lifesaving equipment and its technological advances aided the Society in an important way. By 1869, under Forbes' guidance, the Society boasted a comprehensive vanguard of lifeboat and mortar stations from the North Shore to the islands. Twenty-eight lifeboats waited on shore from the Ipswich River to Smith's Point on Nantucket. Thirty-two surfboats, six dories and five metallic lifeboats joined that fleet. Eleven huts of refuge "generally supplied with fuel and straw, - and sometimes broken into by gunners" still stood sentinel. Ten mortar stations could provide further service to shipwrecked mariners when boats were unable to do the job. In all, ninety-two separate lifesaving stations stood as the front line of the war of man against sea in Massachusetts.

Nonetheless, the Massachusetts Humane Society volunteer lifesaver was about to be reinforced, and eventually replaced. In 1872, the newly-invigorated United States Life-Saving Service constructed nine stations on Cape Cod, signaling the coming end to the Golden Age of the Humane Society's lifesaving operations.

In 1876, while the Life-Saving Service was still under the control of the Revenue Cutter Service and creating its own identity, Forbes continued his work. According to the 1876 *History*, he "put to personal test, at Provincetown and Nantucket, a Rogers life-raft, under consideration by the Society." Colonel Theodore L. Saidley, U.S. Army, joined Forbes, Trustee Caleb Agry Curtis and Captain George Dewey, U.S. Navy, the future hero of the Battle of Manila Bay, in testing rifled guns, "with such success that the great range of five hundred yards has been obtained. If this range can be relied upon, it is probable that rifled guns will be substituted for mortars at such places as Peaked Hill Bars, and others of the more dangerous points along the coast."

By 1877, Forbes had been a Trustee for thirty-six years, the society's second vice president for three years and the first vice president for thirteen more. Unbeknownst to the rest of the Trustees, he coveted the presidency. When he was passed over that year for the Reverend Samuel Kirkland Lothrop, he made a stunning decision, leaving the Humane Society. "I resigned in May, 1877, the Society having at the annual election in April chosen the second vice-president as chief over my head, although he was aware I expected to be elected in regular course."

His efforts on behalf of the shipwrecked mariner were not yet at an end. The *Annual Report of the United States Life-Saving Service, 1890*, noted that "The opinions of a man of his great practical experience were of much value, and during the period of the reorganization of the Life-Saving Service" - the Life-Saving Service broke away from the Revenue Cutter Service in 1878 - "his advice was frequently sought and cheerfully given, to the manifest advantage of the Service. In 1879, upon the appointment of the board to examine and report upon the various types of boats and other similar appliances proposed by inventors for use at the life-saving stations, Captain Forbes was tendered the office of its president, which he accepted. To the duties of this position he brought a wealth of experience and information concerning life-saving devices and other matters coming before the board for discussion, and although the office was without salary Captain Forbes labored earnestly and faithfully for the welfare of the Service, attending all meetings and exhibiting that depth of interest and benevolence of spirit which characterized all his undertakings."

He continued publishing. In 1880, he wrote *The Lifeboat and Other Lifesaving Inventions*; in 1883, *New Rig for Steamers*; and in 1884, *Notes on Navigation*. In 1888, his mind turned towards history, as he penned his last work, *Notes on Ships of the Past*. In 1878, in his autobiography, *Personal Reminiscences*, he summarized the Golden Age of the Humane Society and the role he perceived he played in it.

> At the time of my election, in May 1841, the Society had only eighteen boats and some houses of refuge on the coasts of the State. There are now - including boats and mortar stations, and houses of refuge - eighty-one stations. The apparatus of the Society, although very far from being as complete and well organized as that of similar institutions in England and France, has done much good, and is capable of doing much more. The State has several times contributed considerable sums to its funds; also the General

Government. But the latter, having recently undertaken to establish life-saving stations along the whole coasts of the country, will not be likely to contribute in the future to the Humane Society. The influence of the Society has been evidenced by the establishment of a similar society in New York, as well as in promoting action on the part of government; and I take to myself a fair share of the credit.

Captain Robert Bennett Forbes died in his Milton home at 4:15 p.m. on November 23, 1889. "Few citizens have done greater or nobler work for the welfare of the American seamen than Captain Forbes," read the *Annual Report of the United States Life-Saving Service*. "With a benevolence that was without stint, his active mind was ever bent upon some plan for the amelioration of the hardships of the men who play such an important part in conducting the commerce of the world."

As for final words, Forbes, of course, had his. In the final paragraph of his autobiography, he felt "that it is time to begin to think of that long voyage whence no traveler returns. The only inscription I desire to have on my gravestone is; -

"He Tried To Do His Duty."

Chapter 12:
Forgotten Hero

About one month after the Humane Society had formed, a letter arrived detailing the heroics of a man named Andrew Sloane. In February, 1786, at a meeting held at the home of Dr. John Warren, the trustees voted to reward Sloane with fourteen shillings for saving a boy who had fallen through the ice of a millpond. In October, 1787, they rewarded the savior of a boy who had fallen into a deep cistern and required resuscitation. "Such were the beginnings of a long series of cases," writes Mark Anthony DeWolfe Howe, "amounting to many hundreds in number, which, in their very degrees of human peril and suffering on the one hand, of heroic exertion and humanity on the other, have awakened the sympathies and obtained the premiums of the Society."

The list of reward-worthy lifesaving actions in the annals of the Humane Society is so lengthy that since the middle of the nineteenth century it has consisted of nothing more than a name and either attached dollar figures or the mentioning of a material reward. Yet for every name, there was a moment of terror, at least one life hanging on the edge of expiration. For every $5, there was an extreme physical action, or a quick mental reaction. For every gold, silver or bronze medal, a hero had been born. Most of the details of the stories of the rewards granted by the Humane Society, if they exist at all, rest in the pages of ancient local newspapers, perhaps never to see the light of day again.

While many of the medals and other premiums awarded by the Society were direct results of rescue and resuscitation of potential drowning victims, other actions occasionally merited the attention of the Trustees. In 1865, the Trustees thankfully handed $15 to Cornelius O'Brien of Boston for "his humane efforts in rescuing from smothering in a vault, Richard O. Neil." In 1873, they rewarded Mary Anne Keyes for her strenuous efforts during a disastrous conflagration. "The fire was discovered at 10.06 o'clock on the morning of February 27," writes Arthur Wellington Brayley in *A Complete History of the Boston Fire Department*, "in the mattress factory of Mr. G.A. Sammett, located at the corner of Hanover and Blackstone streets." Three firefighters were killed when a wall collapsed on them, and fourteen more injured. Two young women working inside the building perished in the flames, and a third suffered severe injuries after jumping from a window. Keyes earned a silver medal from the Society "for her courageous and judicious conduct at the late fire on Hanover Street, whereby a number of women were saved from being burned to death, or from serious injury." Keyes led fifteen other girls in escaping from the fourth story of the six-story building, leaping onto the roof of an adjacent structure. She injured herself in the process. On December 22, 1875, William Pepper brought glory to his name when, after a gas explosion destroyed one end of the Federal Street Bridge, he dove into the Fort Point Channel, "rescuing several persons blown into the water."

Medal recipients could perform their actions in Massachusetts, as did John Peabody Gardner in 1860, who saved a young boy from drowning in Back Bay, or in faraway locales, like Seaman John Thomas of the *USS Katahdin*, a Beverly resident who performed the same act on the Mississippi River in 1862 for two fellow sailors. Gardner, a merchant from a prominent Boston family, later became a trustee of the Society.

The Society kept track of its repeat rescuers. In 1867, the Trustees thanked Dudley Davis of Salem for saving the lives of sixteen men and one woman over the stretch of twenty years. George Tewksbury, the "Hero of Deer Island," did him several better. "He has brought up a large family in that vicinity," writes James Lloyd Homer in *Nahant, and Other Places on the Northshore*, "having lived on Deer Island twenty-five or thirty years, during which time his exertions in saving men from drowning were characterized by boldness and energy - and in almost every instance they were crowned with success." But Tewksbury did not always work alone, according to Homer. "In his philanthropic efforts, he has at different times received valuable assistance from members of his family. When I tell you that he and his sons have been the means, under divine favor, of saving between *twenty-five* and *thirty* human beings from a watery grave, you will have some idea of the extent of their labors." The Humane Society's records officially documented thirty-three people saved by 1856. "When the worthy old gentleman dies," continues Homer, "a monument should be erected to his memory, near the scene of his philanthropic and fearless exploits, to remind generations to come that so noble and bold a spirit once lived and breathed in the land."

Joshua James of Hull had already earned a bronze medal from the Society for his part in the rescue of the brig *L'Essai* in 1850 and a certificate for the rescue of the crew of the *Delaware* in 1857 before accepting a specially struck silver medal for forty years of service as a lifesaver in 1886. Before he died in 1902 he would earn a gold medal from the Society for his actions during the gale of November 1888, and another silver medal for his rescue of the crew of the schooner *Ulrica* in 1896.

In 1891, the Society awarded another of its long-term service medals to Edmund Soper Hunt of Weymouth. A fireworks manufacturer by trade, Hunt developed a line-throwing gun when approached by two other inventors in 1877 who were struggling with perfection of their device. His gun, designed to carry a rope to a distant target, and thus practical for use with the Humane Society's breeches buoy rescue system, raised the eyebrows of the Society's Trustees, who arranged for test firings. At one, on Hunt's land in Weymouth, he remembered in his autobiography, "The gentlemen were enthusiastic, and ran like boys across the fields and up the hill where the shot landed." Despite the fact that Robert Bennett Forbes told him that if he had "invented a machine to destroy lives rather than one to save lives, I could have made much money," he pressed

The Humane Society recognized lifesavers and ancillary heroes as well, such as Edmund Soper Hunt, developer of the line-throwing gun shown here being prepared for firing by Society volunteers (Courtesy of Dick Boonisar).

on with the gun's development, granted $500 from the Society to do so. He visited England on behalf of the Society, demonstrating it for British lifesaving officials, and even took part in side-by-side comparisons with the U.S. Life-saving Service's line-throwing gun of choice, the Lyle gun, "where I completely defeated the Government officials with their apparatus." With his gun adopted for use statewide by volunteer lifesaving crews, the Humane Society awarded Hunt its gold medal.

Some rescues drew major media attention. The hybrid steamer *City of Columbus* struck on the ledge known as Devil's Bridge, off the western end of Martha's Vineyard, around 3 a.m. on January 18, 1884, sinking in ten minutes with eighty passengers and forty-five members of its crew. Water rushed into the ship, killing most of the passengers in their cabins within those first few minutes, including all of the women and children. A small percentage of the people on the

Humane Society volunteers up and down the Massachusetts coast lived by one common motto: "I'd like to think that if I was the one who was out there, someone would come for me" (Courtesy of Dick Boonisar).

ship climbed into the rigging, as the ship's two masts remained above water. Some froze to death in place, and others fell into the sea when their strength gave out. Still others held out hope that they would be rescued.

At dawn, Keeper Horatio Pease of the Gay Head Lighthouse coordinated a rescue operation from the shore. The local Wampanoag residents of the island formed a crew - Joseph Peters, Samuel Haskins, Samuel Anthony, James and Moses Cooper and John P. Vanderhoop - and headed toward the wreck in the Humane Society's lifeboat. "In the excitement," writes George A. Hough, Jr., in *Disaster at Devil's Bridge*, "Keeper Pease forgot the life-preservers which the Humane Society provided with its boat. No one else thought of them. One man went barefooted into the lifeboat."

Rowing hard into the face of northwest winds, the crew grimaced as ice formed on their boat. "Spray turned to ice on the clothing of the men at the oars," writes Hough. "They had two and a half miles to go to the masts on Devil's Bridge." Once alongside the vessel, the would-be rescuers had more obstacles to face.

"There was much wreckage thrashing about the stranded steamer, and this, with the constant breaking away of the upper works and the force of the receding waves from the ledge, made it impossible for any boat to get near enough for those in the rigging to be taken directly into it," wrote Gustav Kobbe in *The Century Magazine*. "They were obliged to jump, and many were injured by the wreckage, or so badly disabled that they were drowned before they could reach the boat."

As the first crew returned, exhausted, Pease organized a second. James Mosher, Leonard Vanderhoop, Conrad Jeffers, Patrick Devine, Charles Grimes and Peter Johnson, all Wampanoags as well, rowed to the wreck, transferring survivors from the rigging to the revenue cutter *Samuel Dexter*, which arrived early in the afternoon. Pease then called for the retrieval of a third lifeboat, from Squibnocket, which launched with yet another crew: Eddy L. Flanders, William Mayhew, Elliot C. Mayhew, Benjamin F. Mayhew, William Walker and Cyrus C. Look. The *Dexter* launched boats as well. A whaleboat launched from shore on the sight of floating wreckage swamped and returned to the beach.

After five hours of rescue work, only two men remained in the rigging, apparently unable to make their way down to the lifeboats. After having made two transfers of survivors and bodies from the *Columbus* to the *Dexter*, Lieutenant John U. Rhodes of the Revenue Cutter Service volunteered to swim to the ship and climb the rigging to secure the men. "In his first endeavour he was struck by a piece of floating timber, and had to abandon the attempt," writes Lieutenant Worth G. Ross in *Harper's New Monthly Magazine*. "Although injured, he insisted on making another trial, and succeeded in removing the helpless, half-frozen creatures, both of whom died after reaching a place of safety." In all, despite the heroic efforts of so many men, only twenty-six survivors lived to tell the tale. Twenty of them were rescued in Humane Society lifeboats.

The Humane Society, in a public ceremony, presented Rhodes a gold medal, Captain Eric Gabrielson, commanding *Samuel Dexter*, and Lieutenant Charles D. Kennedy, who manned a second lifeboat from *Dexter*, silver medals, with citations for humane efforts and a total of $200 distributed to the rest of the crew. Each of the twelve

Gay Head men manning the first two lifeboats received silver medals and $25 apiece. The six Chilmark men in the Squibnocket boat, which arrived too late to save any lives, received bronze medals and $15 apiece, and the crew of the swamped whaleboat, Thomas Jeffers, Henry Jeffers, John Lula, Charles Stevens and Simeon Devine, all received certificates and $10 each. Keeper Pease of the lighthouse accepted a certificate and $25 for his efforts that day. Trustee Benjamin W. Crowninshield visited the island to make the presentations, announcing as well that newspapers around the state of Massachusetts had conscripted $3500 and placed it in the charge of the Society for distribution to the Wampanoag community on Martha's Vineyard. The ceremony ended with an exhibition of the Hunt gun.

Some medal-worthy actions, despite grandness in scope, would have gone completely unnoticed if not for the reporting of a lone voice, as in the case of the Galway Line steamer *Connaught*. One survivor notified the *New York Times* as to the heroics of the rescuers after the ship began leaking and then caught fire a hundred and fifty miles east of Boston, on the final leg of its journey from Galway to Boston via St. John's, Newfoundland.

> New York, Saturday, October 13, 1860
> Messrs. Howland & Aspinwall, New York:
>
> Dear Sirs - As one of the nearly six hundred persons saved from the unfortunate Connaught, allow me to address you a few words in behalf of our brave rescuer, Capt. John Wilson, of the brig *Minnie Schiffer*, to whom, under God, we owe our lives.
>
> Sustained, as I believe, by the Almighty, I was enabled to note with calmness the agonizing scenes which occurred on the quarter-deck of the steamship Connaught on Sunday last, the 7th inst., and commence at that point when it was evident to all that now we were, humanly speaking, without hope. Two vessels were seen in the distance, and hope revived. It was soon clear, however, that one of these was passing in the distance, and could not, I think,

possibly see us - our low fore and aft rig aiding this result. The second vessel was soon made out to be a brig, and from her course likely to make us out, as we were slowly reaching ahead under our fore-and-afters, with a Quartermaster at the wheel.

At this time I went forward to the bridge, and was convinced that there was little hope of our being seen, large as our Union down half-mast ensign was. Soon, however, the cry arose, 'She sees us!' and in a short time we could see with the naked eye that the brig had put up her helm and was rushing with bursting canvas, dead before the gale, right for us. In less than half an hour she had passed our weather quarter, near our little fleet of boats, and rounding to to windward, picked up a gig containing one lady and a few others. Still there was doubt as to her intentions, but in a few minutes she wore round, braced up sharp on the other tack, and was soon close to our lee quarter, with her commander assuring us, so far as the gale permitted, or all possible help. We now perceived with grateful hearts, that He who works by human instruments had not only given us the man for our needs in Capt. Leitch, but also raised up in the man now sent to our rescue, the noble fellow Capt. John Wilson, of the *Minnie Schiffer*, has since proved himself to be. Capt. Wilson handled his vessel in the most masterly manner - heaving to pick up our boats with passengers, and then carrying on, under a heavy press of canvas, again to gain the wreck; in some cases - as in that of the writer - not waiting to take passengers in, not towing the boat astern, until he was once more on the steamer's lee quarter. About 6 p.m., when I reached his vessel, Capt. Wilson was so anxious lest the large number still on board would perish before his eyes, that he determined to get a hawser from the steamer, which he at once did, and hung by it for several hours.

In this way much time was saved, and the boat now passed to and from the steamer with great dispatch and regularity, the sea having, most providentially, much gone down.

When we were all on board the little Minnie, Capt. Wilson was devoted to our wants, and seemed to be perfectly happ in the consciousness of having saved us from so dreadful a death.

I trust you will kindly interest yourself in procuring from New-York, and the country at large, a suitable acknowledgement of Capt. Wilson's bravery and humanity.

It will be my official duty to write the State Department on this subject, and I fully expect that the President will make Capt. Wilson a valuable present.

While it seems proper to add that the crew of the brig seemed delighted to aid in our rescue, I cannot omit mention of Mr. Thos. H. Connauton, the mate of the brig, who nobly seconded his commander, and to whose great kindness while on board we are all much indebted.

Very truly yours,
W.H. Newman
U.S. Consul at St. Johns, Newfoundland.

The Humane Society rewarded Captain Wilson with a gold medal, Mate Connauton a silver medal, and $10 to each member of the *Minnie Schiffer's* crew.

The appearance of a rescue crew when all seemed lost raised one's spirits from the depths of despair to utter elation. Edward K. Godfrey wrote in *The Island of Nantucket, What It Was and What It Is* about the wreck of the schooner *Mary Anna* on February 4, 1871. "Her situation was discovered at daylight, and the 'Island Home' was sent to her assistance, but was unable to reach her on account of the ice, which completely obstructed her way and forced her to remain just outside of Brant Point for three days. But here was this vessel full of water, mercury below zero, and seven men in the rigging who must be saved. A crew of eight men, after almost superhuman efforts, succeeded at last, with the aid of a board and a dory, in getting to the vessel."

Arthur H. Gardner, in *Wrecks around Nantucket*, mentions two dories. "The night was clear, but the air was stinging cold and the ice in some places unfit to bear the weight of the dories. At such places the boards came into play and in two instances they were obliged to take to their boats and pull. Thus altering the means of locomotion to suit the circumstances, they toiled on some two hours and a half in passing a distance of about two miles."

"The captain afterwards said when he saw these men coming to his rescue," continues Godfrey, "there seemed to be a halo about their heads, such as is represented in the pictures of our Saviour; that he had read of the angel of mercy, but never until now had he realized the full force of the expression."

The eight men, Isaac Hamblin, George A. Veeder, Alexander Fanning, James A. Holmes, Joseph P. Gardner, William E. Bates, Stephen Keyes and Henry C. Coffin, each received a silver medal and $10 from the Humane Society.

By the end of the nineteenth century, the name Humane Society of the Commonwealth of Massachusetts had become synonymous with heroism, bravery and compassion for human life. Hundreds of rescuers had been recognized for saving the lives of thousands of innocent victims of disasters, some individually, others in large groups. After a century of continuous operation, despite natural changes to the makeup of the Board of Trustees through time, the original mission of the Society to preserve human life was certainly being achieved.

Chapter 13:
The Price

"They that go down to the sea in ships, that do business in great waters," according to the Psalms, understand that they do so at a self-imposed peril. The same sea that calmly offers its bounty for personal or commercial gain can turn deadly in minutes. In times of distress, a sea captain's options include dropping an anchor and riding out a storm, or running for port. For centuries, the rewards have been worth the risk for generations of fishermen and freight haulers alike.

The volunteer lifesaver of the Humane Society and the "government's hired man" of the Life-Saving Service were expected to look the dangers of the sea in the face and meet them head on. When gales were at their worst and lives were imperiled on the sea, they entered wooden crafts a tenth the size of the ships being torn apart by the storms and manually willed themselves to the rescue. Sadly, despite following the best safety precautions and donning the most up-to-date life-preserving equipment of the time, not all of them came back alive.

On the night of February 24, 1893, the captain of the British brig *Aquatic*, heading from Cuba to Boston, unwittingly ran his vessel aground on Sow and Pigs Reef, between the shore and the lightship that shared the reef's name. "It was a stormy night, bitter cold with snow and sleet, and a dangerous sea was breaking over the rocks," states *The Sailors' Magazine and Seamens' Friend*. "Signals of distress

To the lifeboat hero came the spoils: fame, medals and more. But on occasion the risks proved too great, and lifesavers lost their lives attempting to save others (Courtesy of Dick Boonisar).

were sent out from the wreck." The island, the last in the Elizabeth Island chain at the entrance to Buzzards Bay, was well-equipped to respond to the wreck. A lighthouse stood overlooking the reef at the western end of the island, where the Humane Society kept two of its boats. The United States Life-Saving Service had built a station at the eastern end of the island, overlooking Canapitsit Channel, in 1889. The Humane Society volunteers from Station Number 43 were closer to the wreck than their federally paid counterparts, and reacted first.

"A lifeboat commanded by Captain Timothy Akin and manned by five volunteers," continues the magazine article, "who responded to his call, went out to the brig, but not without remonstrance from the more cautious veterans of the cliffs. It seemed indeed a foolhardy errand. Even if the lifeboat could succeed in reaching the vessel, a rescue in such a sea and with the breakers surging around the wreck was hardly practicable."

"Slowly she staggered forward," wrote Arthur Cleveland Hall in *New England Magazine*, "up and down amid the waves. Captain Tim was a man who never knew fear. 'Come on boys, - ain't this fun!' he shouted from his place at the steering oar." But the fun ended abruptly. Just alongside the brig, Captain Akin called for a line to be thrown down to the lifeboat, but before it could be secured, a gigantic rolling wave turned the boat over. "Two of the oarsmen sank to the bottom without a struggle," noted *The Sailors' Magazine and Seamens' Friend*. "Two clung for a few minutes to the bottom of the boat and were then swept away."

The captain reached out to the last remaining man, Joseph Tilton, who could not swim, with an oar. Using a line lowered from the brig, the sailors hauled Tilton to the deck. When they turned back to bring the captain aboard, he was gone. The following day, after the storm abated, the Life-Saving Service crew safely removed all of the sailors and Tilton from the brig. Captain Timothy Akin, Jr., Frederick Akin, Isaiah H. Tilton, William Brightman and Hiram Jackson had all been lost.

The Humane Society faced, for the first time, the deaths of men endeavoring to do good deeds in the name of the organization. The cry went out across the region for support for the wives and now fatherless children, all twelve of them, of the lost lifesavers. The popular subscription that followed raised a sum of $26,702.52, which was handed to the Society for distribution to the families. "More than $10,000 was subscribed to the Society direct," writes Mark Anthony DeWolfe Howe in *The Humane Society of the Commonwealth of Massachusetts*. "Other agencies of collection brought in larger and smaller amounts. The Canadian Government, the Boston Chamber of Commerce, and Boston Stock Exchange made separate contributions, from $1000 downwards." As the ship was registered to St. John, New Brunswick, the Canadian government felt it should find a way to pay respect to the efforts of the Humane Society's volunteers. The Humane Society awarded its gold medal to Joseph Tilton.

Just nine years later, tragedy struck the Massachusetts coast a second time. On Tuesday, March 11, 1902, the barge *Wadena* stranded on Shovelful Shoal, off Monomoy Island at the southern end of the outer arm of Cape Cod. The crew of the Monomoy Lifesaving Station rescued the crew, bringing them securely ashore. A wrecking crew soon ventured out to the wreck, hoping to salvage whatever could be taken to the beach. On March 16, a second storm brewed, and all but five of the wreckers returned to safety aboard the tugboat *Peter Smith*. The crew of the lifesaving station, who had been vigilantly watching the stranded ship, did not realize that the tug had left anybody behind.

The following morning, Captain Marshall W. Eldredge walked to the point, noted a distress flag flying atop the vessel, and called his number one surfman, Seth Ellis, instructing him to launch the station's surfboat from the western side of the island and to pick him up on the row south. "The wind was fresh and there was a heavy sea running, but all the crew were of the opinion that the condition of the barge Wadena was not perilous, as she seemed to be sound and lying easy," Seth Ellis stated later. In rough but tolerable seas, the crew pulled alongside the barge.

The men aboard the ship were desirous of being taken ashore, despite the stability of the vessel. They secured a line to a mast and lowered it over the side, using it to shimmy down into the surfboat. The first four men handled that task efficiently. The fifth, the captain, a heavy man, fell hard on the aft section of the surfboat, breaking the thwart. Eldredge and his crew pushed off and headed for shore.

"Before we could get the boat turned around a big wave struck us with fearful force, and quite a lot of water poured into the surf-boat," said Ellis. "As soon as the water came into the boat, the rescued men jumped up, and becoming panic-stricken, threw their arms about the necks of the surfmen so that none of us could use our oars. The seas, one after another, struck us, and the boat, filling with water, turned bottom up, throwing us all into the raging sea."

The seas dragged the five men who had been successfully pulled from the barge to their deaths instantly. The lifesaving crew righted the boat once, then twice, then began to lose strength. When the boat capsized a third time, the lifesavers started to succumb to their fates. Surfman Osborn Chase disappeared first, followed by Valentine Nickerson and Edgar Small. Elijah Kendrick and Isaac Foye died next.

Ellis and the station keeper, Marshall Eldredge, clung to one end of the overturned surfboat, while Arthur Rogers kept himself alive at the other end. A tremendous blast of water knocked them all loose. Ellis regained his position, "and looking around for Captain Eldredge, I saw that he was holding onto the spar and sail which had drifted from underneath the boat, but was still fast to it. The seas were washing me off the boat continuously at this time, and when I last saw our brave captain, he was drifting away from the boat, holding on to the spar and sail."

Ellis and Rogers held fast to the boat. Rogers called to Ellis for aid in getting a better hold, but with his own strength sapped, Ellis could only offer encouragement that they would soon be swept to the beach. Rogers said feebly, "I have got to go," and disappeared beneath the waves.

As the overturned boat continued to drift, it passed a second stranded barge, the *Fitzpatrick*. Recognizing the direness of the situation, a wrecker aboard the barge, Elmer F. Mayo, tossed a dory onto the sea and rowed to Ellis' rescue. Skillfully maneuvering his way through the breakers, he landed the dory on the beach in sight of Surfman Walter Bloomer, who had been left behind to man the station. With the rest of the crew dead, Ellis became the keeper of the station, and young Bloomer was designated his number one man.

Upon hearing the news of the tragedy, the Humane Society immediately called for the collection of a fund to take care of the families of the seven lost men. The people of Boston and vicinity raised $36,286.40 by May 28 to aid the widows and children. The Society awarded Mayo its gold medal.

Disastrously, two days after the Monomoy tragedy, on March 19, 1902, a third incident that would lead to the creation of the third special fund in less than a decade unfolded. Learning of the Monomoy tragedy, Keeper Joshua James of the Point Allerton Life-saving Station in Hull, the most decorated lifesaver in American history, ordered his crew out on an unplanned lifeboat drill. The station had recently received a new self-bailing, self-righting surfboat, and he had trepidations regarding his crew's ability to handle it in a situation similar to the one that claimed the Monomoy crew without proper training. On that cold morning, the crew launched their new boat and performed for about an hour.

At the end of that hour, James praised the crew for their work and the boat for its stability and maneuverability. The crew pulled the boat ashore, and the captain leapt out, remarking that the tide had started to ebb. With those final words, he fell insensibly upon the sands, dead before his crew could carry him across the roadway to the station. He was 75 years old.

James' wife Louisa was blind and living at home with three grown daughters. With the Monomoy Fund receiving the lion's share of the incoming contributions at the time, the new Joshua James Fund only raised $3723.68. James was so poor he was buried in the Hull cemetery without a headstone. Several years later, the Society paid for one for him, bearing their seal.

The inherent risks in rescuing lives of sailors in jeopardy on the sea were always readily apparent to the men of Cuttyhunk, Monomoy and Hull, as well as Newburyport, Plymouth and Nantucket. For the most part, the lifesavers themselves had grown up on the shorelines they protected, either as volunteers or paid surfmen. Death in the sea was not inevitable for a Humane Society lifesaver, but it was a possibility.

The triple tragedies of 1893 and 1902 impressed upon the Trustees a new role. As Howe states, it could not "have been foreseen that the beneficence of the Society would go beyond the shipwrecked and include the surviving dependents of their rescuers." In a twist on the words of the Roman poet Juvenal, "*Quis custodiet ipsos custodes*?" the Society learned that on their watch, it was their duty to watch over the watchmen who watched over the sea.

Chapter 14:
End of an Era

The timing of the death of Joshua James could not have been more poetic, more reflective of societal change. The grand old man of American lifesaving had reigned over the era of wooden ships and canvas sails, of the accelerated growth of the cities of the East Coast driven by the Industrial Revolution and a long period of general stasis in the methods of lifesaving employed by shore-based rescuers of mariners imperiled on the sea.

Long before Joshua James was born, Boston Lighthouse on Little Brewster Island became the first light station in the New World, a mile and a quarter from Hull's northern rocky shore. For the entirety of his lifetime, ships hoping to enter the port of Boston passed between Boston Light and the Hull shoreline, navigating narrow, winding and shallow Lighthouse Channel. In 1900, dredging began on a new wider, straighter, deeper passage into the harbor. In 1905, with the lighting of Graves Lighthouse, more than two miles from Hull's Stony Beach, the heaviest traffic entering the harbor moved farther away from the town's lifesavers than it had ever been.

The deeper channel was dredged to meet the demands of a growing fleet, one that was expanding not in number of ships, but in the size of the ships being built. The never-ending production of wooden ships that characterized the years leading up to the War of 1812 came to a crashing halt during the build-up to that conflict, and never regained its steam. Capital moved from the sea to the newest mode of freight transport, the railroad. Those ships that were built began using metals, first at strategic engineering points, then finally as basic construction materials. Motive power techniques moved from the harnessing of wind to internal combustion. In Joshua James' final years, the sight of a tug pulling a string of two or three flat barges that had minimum ability to drive themselves became commonplace, in place of the sight of schooners, barks, brigs and other traditional sailing crafts. Fewer ships could carry the same amount of cargo as a greater number from the days of Joshua's youth.

In 1899, the United States Life-Saving Service began experimentation with a motorized lifeboat on Lake Superior. While steam had made headways into the design of larger vessels, the unwieldiness of the power plants necessary to drive a standard sized lifeboat made it an impossible alternative drive source. The development of small naphtha and gasoline engines allowed for the Marquette tests under Revenue Cutter Service Lieutenant Charles McLellan and Marquette station keeper Henry Cleary. By 1905, the Life-Saving Service had plans to utilize motor lifeboats throughout the United States. A few years later, the Humane Society introduced its first power dory, at Nahant, and added two motor lifeboats in the coming decade, at Hull and Rockport. "The Rockport boat," said Mark Anthony DeWolfe Howe in *The Humane Society of the Commonwealth of Massachusetts*, "thirty feet long, self-bailing, self-righting, designed by Mr. Arthur Binney, of Boston, has her propeller ingeniously placed in a sort of tunnel under the after portion of the craft, so that she can be beached without injury to the blades - a device afterward found to have been applied in English life-boats built at about the same time. At the present moment a boat of this type is building for use at the Society's Cohasset Station - chosen in anticipation of increased need for help when the Cape Cod Canal draws its full share of coastwise traffic from the longer route heretofore unavoidable."

Developments of communication technologies shortened distances for Life-Saving Service surfmen on patrol and their brethren at the stations as motors had done for lifeboats heading to wrecks. While telegraphs had been in place for several decades, the Spanish-American War forced the spreading of telephone lines to lookout points along the coast in the summer of 1898, including Life-Saving Service stations. Keepers received orders to stay on duty throughout that summer with partial crews and to watch for Spanish warships on the horizon. Telephones could deliver the news more quickly and efficiently than ever.

The nature of the Massachusetts coastline had changed as well by 1902. First seen as the stronghold of the rugged New England fisherman, by the end of the nineteenth century, the coast became the domain of the summer reveler and second home owner, a byproduct of the economic class division brought on by the Industrial Revolution. The barren stretches of sand that once called for the erection of lonely houses of refuge were, by 1902, lined with summer cottages, beachfront amusements and passing railroad lines. The state's population in 1790, shortly after the formation of the Society, was 378,787; in 1840, when the Society made its concerted effort to create a system of lifeboat stations along the coast, it was 737,699; in 1900, there were more than 2.8 million people who called Massachusetts home. In 1826, when Joshua James was born, 125 people resided in Hull; on the 4th of July, 1898, 50,000 people celebrated the holiday on Nantasket Beach.

"It should be clearly understood," writes Howe, "that the extension of the Government Life-Saving Service, and the coincident processes of lining the New England coast with summer dwellings and thereby diminishing its desolate character, have by no means rendered the work of the Society in the field of its pioneer effort superfluous or half-hearted. The tendency has been rather to intensify the endeavor to bring the quality of service rendered by the life-saving stations to the highest attainable point."

That said, Howe understood that the trends showed the Golden Era of the Humane Society volunteer lifesaver was coming to an end. "Year by year," he writes, "the total number of stations has shrunk - from the 92 recorded in 1869 to only 36 at the beginning of 1916. The huts of refuge - 11 in 1869 - dwindled by degrees to one, on Tom Nevers Hill, Nantucket, and now for some years that has not appeared on the list."

The world that needed the Humane Society of the Commonwealth of Massachusetts to build huts of refuge, lifeboats

The wreck of the five-masted schooner Nancy on Nantasket Beach in February 1927 proved to be one of the final high profile rescue performed by Humane Society lifeboat crews (Courtesy of Dick Boonisar).

and mortar stations had changed, even disappeared. Even the Life-Saving Service was feeling the sting. The opening of the Cape Cod Canal in 1914 changed already dwindling traffic patterns off Cape Cod, reducing the need for the federal government to pay seven or eight men at thirteen stations to be on guard for ten to twelve months per year. In 1916, in reaction to former President William Howard Taft's push for "unifunctionalism" in federal departments, the Life-Saving Service merged with the Revenue Cutter Service to become the Coast Guard, under the direction of President Woodrow Wilson.

But the Humane Society's volunteers did not lay down their oars and walk away from the shore with the death of Joshua James. They continued their work, in dwindling roles, for a few more decades, punctuating their worth with a grand exit, a final dramatic rescue.

On February 19, 1927, the five-masted schooner *Nancy* ran into a snowstorm shortly after clearing the entrance to Boston Harbor. Her captain, E.M. Baird, ordered the anchors dropped off an offshore ledge, hopeful of riding out the storm in place. "During the night, the anchor chain broke and it first looked as though she would go aground on Harding's Ledge," recounted volunteer lifesaver Arthur Hurley, "but the Captain ordered the staysail set and the ship was worked to clear the Ledge, only to come aground at Nantasket Beach about 100 yards off-shore with eight men aboard."

The ship, as heavy as it was, would not move for a decade, becoming a seaside attraction for nearly the duration of the Great Depression, but at the moment, the locals feared for the lives of the men aboard the ship. The Humane Society lifesavers beat the Coast Guard to the scene, enlisting the help of two horses to drag the surfboat *Nantasket* to the scene of the stranding through a foot of snow. The call went out for volunteers, and nine men stepped forward. The lifesavers attached a line to the surfboat, leaving the other end ashore, as a crowd gathered on the beach.

"The waves were monstrous," writes Hurley, "but the men succeeded in bringing the life boat to the side of the ship which was broadside to the sea. The ship had about thirty feet of freeboard so a rope was put over the side and every time a wave hit the Nancy, she would keel over and dump gallons of water into the life boat. This kept the men very busy bailing out." One man refused to let go of the rope and had to be manhandled by the lifeboat crew. At a given signal, the 200 people ashore who could wrap their hands about it grasped the line and pulled the lifeboat to the beach. "It was very fortunate that the boat was pulled in on a receding wave which gave the men time to get out. The next wave coming in smashed the life boat against the rocky shore. If the life boat had come in on an incoming wave, many lives would have been lost."

The last great Humane Society rescue had been enacted by Adelbert Nickerson, Edwin Hatch, Robert W. Blossom, Clifton Jaeger, Joseph James, James H. Murphy, John J. Sullivan and Hurley, all led by Captain Osceola James, the lone surviving son of Joshua James.

Captain Osceola James, the only surviving son of Joshua James, fittingly performed one of the last Humane Society lifeboat rescues when he led his crew to the Nancy *in 1927 (Courtesy of Dick Boonisar).*

Epilogue

I n his 1918 history of the Society, Mark Anthony DeWolfe Howe noted that the founders "saw in their child untold possibilities of service to mankind; and [that] their vision has been fulfilled." Howe's observation remains true to the present day.

Initially, the Society focused its efforts on the resuscitation of those on the verge of death by drowning or from other causes. Over time the Trustees began to look more broadly at the need for facilities to ensure the preservation of life and the relief of suffering and in so doing, the Society lent support and financial assistance toward the founding of Massachusetts General Hospital, McLean Hospital and the Boston Lying-In Hospital.

The next great venture undertaken by the Society was rescuing shipwrecked mariners whose lives were at risk while navigating the rocky shoreline of Massachusetts Bay and the treacherous shoals lying off Cape Cod and the Islands. It is to this glorious chapter in the Society's history that the current volume is primarily dedicated.

However, by the late 1920s the last power lifeboat built by the Humane Society for use in Cohasset and put into service in 1918 was decommissioned. The era of volunteer life-saving crews drew to a close in the United States. In 1946 the Society disposed of its last remaining life-saving equipment in Marblehead.

Once again, the Trustees turned for guidance to their Charter and found inspiration for new ways to help preserve life and relieve human suffering. After thoughtful consideration, the Trustees redirected their energies and resources on two primary objectives:

>   1. The granting of medals and awards to men and women who without regard for themselves and with bravery help to save the lives of others; and
>   2. The making of grants to charitable organizations engaged in a wide variety of activities aimed at preserving human life and relieving suffering.

The Humane Society had always recognized persons who by singular exertion had helped to save the life of another human being, however this mission was now reinforced and expanded. A Standing Committee was established to identify rescues worthy of consideration. From 1918 until 1949, Ellery H. Clark served as Secretary to the Standing Committee to assist them. Clark was succeeded for a time by Alexander Houston until Mrs. Leroy J. Mann assumed full responsibility for the investigation of rescues in addition to regular secretarial duties. After 25 years of dedicated service, Mrs. Mann retired and was succeeded by Mrs. Barbara Driscoll. Mrs. Driscoll discharged these duties with great skill and what is more Mrs. Driscoll's calligraphy set a standard for the minute book which it is doubtful will ever be exceeded.

Upon the retirement of Barbara Driscoll, the Humane Society Trustees were extremely fortunate to be able to retain the services of Ms. Elizaneth Nilsson who has become an indispensable assistant to the Trustees. With the passage of time the identification and investigation of rescues has become a virtual full-time job. Somehow Ms. Nilsson has managed not only to get the administrative work done to a very high standard but also to provide the Trustees with a careful review of all rescues and grant requests form sundry organizations seeking financial support. Ms. Nilsson's willingness to extend herself well beyond the call of duty led the Trustees to appoint her their Executive Director.

In their periodic reports of the Society, one can find detailed descriptions of each of the rescues for which medals, certificates and monetary awards have been conferred. Among these are those rescues deemed worthy of the William Penn Harding Award which is reserved for those who have demonstrated "unselfish bravery in saving or attempting to save another in extreme peril of death by drowning or by fire during the year previous to the award." The Trustees hold regular scheduled lunch and dinner meetings to review the rescues that have been identified and investigated by the Executive Director and recommended by the Standing Committee. Whenever possible, medals are awarded to the rescuer(s) in person by one or more of the Trustees.

The factual rescue summaries which accompany each and every recommendation from the Standing Committee can be extremely dramatic. For example:

> Eighteen year old John Cacaccio, a junior and an honor student at Norton High School was driving along Rt. 140 on the morning of January 19, 2017, when he saw an SUV floating in Norton Reservoir. He immediately stopped, called 911 as he was running and jumped into the frigid water and swam about 40 feet to the vehicle where he found the driver struggling and disoriented. John checked to see if anyone else was in the SUV. The driver was alone. Then John attempted to swim the driver to shore, and convince him that he would be all right, but the driver panicked and started swimming further away shouting, "No! No!" John stayed with the victim, holding onto to him, inching to shore, and telling him that he would be okay and that help was arriving. The driver was very agitated and continued struggling. Within minutes the firefighters were on the scene and the 51-year-old driver was rescued. He was taken to Sturdy Memorial Hospital in Attleboro and was treated for hypothermia. Once on shore John was wrapped in a blanket and examined by the paramedics. He did not need to go to the hospital.

Police Chief Brian Clark said the water temperature was estimated to be in the 30's and there was a thin film of ice on the water. He went on to say, "John Cacaccio acted quickly and courageously swimming to the SUV, making sure no one else was in the vehicle and helping the driver until the firefighters arrived."

Sometimes medals are awarded for highly publicized rescues where the media has already identified and heralded the rescuer in the local press and, perhaps, interviewed the hero or heroine on television and radio. However, quite often rescuers prefer to avoid publicity and keep their stories to themselves. They feel that what they did to save a life was only what was to be expected of them under the circumstances. They are, indeed, true heroes. One Trustee told a story of the difficulty he experienced in persuading two men in his neighborhood who had rescued two kayakers from certain death by drowning in the mouth of the Annisquam River to accept silver medals for their achievement.

Soon after joining this amazing group, I mentioned to a friend that I was now part of a group that gave awards for bravery in rescue. He told me of a recent rescue of two kayakers at the mouth of the Annisquam River in rough seas by two local men, both of whom I knew. In my first encounter with "reluctant heroes," Brad "Dirt" Murray and Doug Ritchie finally agreed to a quiet ceremony on my lawn in Annisquam. I was accompanied by Trustees Prout and Saltonstall. Shortly after we began, several others arrived: David Murray (Dirt's father, who had earned the Society silver medal twice), Curtis Murray (Dirt's brother, who had earned it once) and Mike Standley (a friend who had earned it once alongside David Murray in one of his rescues). It was an unique moment to have them all together at the same time, men of the sea who rose to the occasion when needed.

132

Over the years, the Trustees have made grants to worthy organizations for causes that satisfy the broad purposes for which the Society was founded. Among others, grants have been made to some of the leading hospitals in the community, including Massachusetts General Hospital, McLean Hospital and other diversions of the Harvard Medical School complex of Teaching Hospitals. In addition, the Trustees have supported swimming and lifesaving programs given by the Red Cross, the Boy Scouts and the YMCA. Concern for water safety has also led the Society to furnish life-saving equipment and to support related programs at Thompson Academy Outward Bound on Thompson's Island in Boston Harbor. The Trustees provided both Thompson Academy and Hurricane Island Outward Bound with boats that have been custom-designed for their educational programs aimed at teaching young people basic boat-handling skills. Pursuant to its mission, the Trustees have made grants to Boston MedFlight to provide their helicopter pilots with up-to-date GPS technology and with night vision goggles. Grants have also been made to the Coast Guard Auxiliary to supply their patrols with cutting edge radio and other communication equipment. The Societies' grant making has even been extended to such purely humanitarian causes such as The Samaritans, Freedom from Chemical Dependency and the NAACP for social welfare programs.

When considering grant requests, the Trustees are alert to the possibility of leveraging their grants with other donors and seek to determine whether the program they are being asked to support can be put on a self-sustaining basis.

Lest it be thought that the Trustees are no longer concerned about those who make their living on the water, the Trustees helped to fund a study into fishing boat safety conducted by Woods Hole Oceanographic Research Center and have supported the Gloucester Fishermen's Alliance in furnishing safety gear for fishermen which allows for easy movement and provides flotation in the event of an emergency. Furthermore, the Trustees maintain a close working relationship with the First District Coast Guard Commander and his staff and encourage their work in a variety of ways.

For many years after the Society was founded, the Trustees were mostly prosperous Boston merchants and ship owners. As of the early twenty-first century, the Trustees are still white males with Boston connections. They have proven to be civic minded, thoughtful, generous and at the same time collegial and simply fond of each other's company. One Trustees, Charles Devens, said that over a long and highly successful life he felt that the Trustees of the Humane Society of the Commonwealth of Massachusetts was the group that he most admired and enjoyed. This seems to be a continuing sentiment.

Since the Society's founding the Trustees have tried, whenever possible to hold their meetings at the houses of a fellow Trustee in a regular rotation. This custom sprang from a time when most of the Trustees resided in or near the City of Boston. More recently the Trustees have been required to hold some of their meetings at a variety of other locations. However, they do their best to uphold the best of the traditions established by their predecessors including the time-honored standing toast "To All Humane Societies,"

The Trustees of the Humane Society of the Commonwealth of Massachusetts, 2016. Front row; left to right: W. Nicholas Thorndike, Lawrence T. Perera. Back row; left to right: H.D.S. Greenway, Ian H. Gardiner, George Lewis, G. West Saltonstall, David T. Lawrence, Robert T. Osteen, Ross E. Sherbrooke. Missing: Henry P. Becton, Jr., Ferdinand Colloredo-Mansfeld, Edward P. Lawrence.

made at the conclusion of dinner which is accompanied by the raising of a glass of Madeira. In this way continuity has been maintained with the era when virtually all the Trustees were Boston merchants, ship owners and retired sea captains. In recognition of the current trend toward informality it must be noted that the Trustees now wear black tie instead of white to dinner meetings. The sartorial change only occasioned the resignation of one of their most senior members.

Dr. Curt Prout recalled an evening when he drove Humane Society President Leverett Saltonstall to a dinner meeting in the white tie era. Along the way, Dr. Prout stopped to pay a house call to a

patient in Brookline. President Saltonstall asked if he might accompany Prout on the call, which he did from time to time with his father-in-law who was also a physician. Accordingly, the two Trustees attired in white tie entered a small apartment on Beacon Street in Brookline much to the amusement of Dr. Pout's patient who did not expect such a high standard of dress for a routine house call.

The Trustees continue to be persons who have demonstrated success in their respected callings and a deep concern for the civic and charitable well-being of the community. Many of them have more than a casual acquaintance with seafaring. They are well aware of the hazards and challenges that face those made their living from the sea. Rescues of those at risk of drowning rank at the top of their priority for the awarding of medals. The Trustees remain ever mindful of their motto taken from the Book of Exodus, Chapter II, verse X, which is inscribed on their official seal: "He drew him out of the water."

In conclusion, it is appropriate to remember one of the Humane Society's most distinguished Trustees. John Endicott Lawrence was first elected a Trustee in 1948 and served as its President from 1979 to 1993. He loved all the institutions he served as well: the United States Navy, Massachusetts General Hospital and Groton School among them. His interest in the sea, rowing and local history were instrumental in the establishment of the Hull Lifesaving Museum. His peers loved him. He, in turn, gave respect and love to others. As Hamlet said of his father, "There was a man. Take it all in all; we shall not look upon his like again."

It was President Lawrence who inspired the Trustees to commission this new history of the Humane Society and it is to him and his memory that this book is dedicated.

Postscript:
USCGC Joshua James

More than a century after his passing, Joshua James remained in the news.

In 2010, the Coast Guard released its official list of the top ten Coast Guard rescues of all time. The list potentially included all events from 1790 forward, at lighthouses, from cutters, helicopters, small boats, the Revenue Cutter Service and the Life-Saving Service. Narrowing down the list – for instance, the Life-Saving Service had been credited with saving 186,000 lives during its 47 year history – was a harrowing task, but in the end, several obvious and exemplary efforts stood out.

Fresh in the minds of the Coast Guard's list compilers was the Hurricane Katrina effort, a massive undertaking:

> Search and rescue operations alone saved 24,135 lives from imminent danger, usually off the roofs of the victims' homes as flood waters lapped at their feet. Coast Guardsmen "evacuated to safety" 9,409 patients from local hospitals. In total, 33,545 lives were saved. Seventy-six Coast Guard and Coast Guard Auxiliary aircraft took part in the rescues. They flew 1,817 sorties with a total flight time of 4,291.3 hours in the air. The air crews saved 12,535. A total of 42

cutters and 131 small boats also participated, with their crews rescuing 21,200. More than 5,000 Coast Guardsmen served in Katrina operations.

In second place was the rescue of the *Prinsendam*, 130 miles off the Alaskan coast in October 1980. The Coast Guard, acting jointly with the Canadian Coast Guard, rescued all 520 people aboard the stricken Dutch cruise liner. Third in the judging was the February 1952 rescue of the crew of the T-2 tanker *Pendleton* off Chatham, Massachusetts, led by Boatswain's Mate First Class Bernard C. Webber, a story later made into a movie by Disney. In fourth place was the World War II tale of the transport *Dorchester*, torpedoed by a U-boat. The cutters *Escanaba* and *Comanche* responded and saved 230 men from imminent death in the frigid sea.

In fifth place of the top ten Coast Guard rescues of all time was the remarkable effort of Joshua James and his team of Hull lifesavers during the Great Storm of 1888:

> Joshua James and the Hull, Mass., Life Saving Station (Nov. 25-26, 1888). Over the two day period, Keeper Joshua James and his crew, by their zealous and unswerving work, rescued some 28 people from five different vessels during a great storm. In addition to the number of individuals rescued, the number of vessels involved, the weather conditions, and the duration of their efforts, James and his crew conducted differing types of rescues which included the employment of the beach apparatus and rescue by boat. For their versatility, endurance, skill, and dedication, James and his crew were awarded the Gold Lifesaving Medal.

While it was a fantastic honor, it was slightly misplaced; Joshua James was not a member of the United States Life-Saving Service in 1888, as the Point Allerton Life-Saving Station had not yet been built. He was the keeper of the Humane Society's boat and mortar stations.

But there was more to come. Two years before the formation of the list, in February, 2008, the Coast Guard sent the first of its new National Security Cutters, USCGC *Bertholf*, out for sea trials. The cutter acquisition program, according to the service,

> addresses the Coast Guard's need for open-ocean patrol cutters with the seakeeping, habitability, endurance and technological advancement to serve as command and control centers in the most demanding maritime environments. Each NSC is built to serve as operational-level headquarters for complex law enforcement, defense and national security missions involving Coast Guard and multiple partner agency participation. The NSCs feature advanced command, control, communication, computers, intelligence, surveillance and reconnaissance equipment; aviation support facilities; stern cutter boat launch; and long-endurance station keeping.

The further need the cutters addressed was that of an aging fleet. The service's 378-foot Hamilton-class high endurance cutters had been in service since the 1960s and were losing their effectiveness in a world in which new technologies appeared every day. The National Security Cutters would bring the Coast Guard's deep water capabilities into the twenty-first century.

More than that, they would instill pride in the men and women who served aboard them. Also known as the Legends Class, the cutters would be named for the few individuals the Coast Guard looked to as its ultimate heroes. The first cutter would carry the name of Ellsworth Bertholf, the first "Captain-Commandant" of the Coast Guard upon its 1915 creation from the Revenue Cutter Service and Life-Saving Service. The second bore the name of Admiral Russell R. Waesche, the service's Commandant in World War II, and the third was named in honor of Captain Dorothy L. Stratton, the head of the Coast Guard women's auxiliary, the SPARS, during the same war. The fourth, USCGC Hamilton, celebrated the legacy of Alexander Hamilton,

Secretary of the Treasury, under whose watch the Revenue Cutter Service came into being in 1790.

The fifth National Security Cutter was named for Joshua James.

The *James'* keel was laid by Ingalls Shipbuilding in Pascagoula, Mississippi, on May 17, 2013, and the cutter was launched for its sea trials on May 3, 2014. A little more than a year later, on August 8, 2015, the USCGC *Joshua James*, hull number WMSL-754, appeared in Boston Harbor for its commissioning. "Joshua James began his life-saving career at 15 and saved more than 600 lives," said service commandant Adm. Paul Zukunft during the ceremony. "What better namesake for a ship and crew that will serve our Nation with pride for the next half century saving lives, stopping smugglers, maintaining safety and security in the Arctic and wherever national objectives may require."

Showing respect for the long history of Joshua James and what he means to the people of Massachusetts, the Coast Guard invited members of the Humane Society Board of Trustees to attend the commissioning.

After the ceremony, the cutter headed for its new homeport of Charleston, South Carolina, taking with it a little bit of the history of the Humane Society of the Commonwealth of Massachusetts.

Acknowledgments

The author would like to thank the Trustees of the Humane Society of the Commonwealth of Massachusetts for their dedication to the promulgation of their institutional history, with particular thanks extended to Lawrence T. Perera and the late Curtis Prout, M.D., overseers of this project. He would also like to thank Elizabeth Nilsson, Executive Director of the Humane Society, for her untiring work in support of this project, and her wonderful sense of the small touches needed to make a book just right.

Beyond the doors of the Humane Society is a world of historians dedicated to telling its tale, including Dick Boonisar of Sandwich; Maurice Gibbs and Jeremy Slavitz of Nantucket; Richard Cleverly of Hull, as well as the staff of the Hull Lifesaving Museum; Captain W. Russell Webster, United States Coast Guard (Retired); David Ball and Fred Freitas of the Scituate Historical Society; Life-Saving Service historians Ralph Shanks, Fred Stonehouse and Dennis Noble; Coast Guard historians Scott Price and Bill Thiesen; the regents and officers of the Foundation for Coast Guard History; the members of the United States Life-Saving Service Heritage Association; and the many volunteers working at the coastal historical societies from Martha's Vineyard to the Merrimac River.

We are indebted, too, for the right to use the magnificent work of John Kilroy on our cover, his painting of the Surfboat *Nantasket*. It truly captures the spirit of the Golden Age of the Humane Society lifesaver.

Made in the USA
Middletown, DE
26 April 2019